Texts: Filippo Salviati, Sergio Basso
Project director: Cinzia Caiazzo
Editor-in-chief: Filippo Melli
Design: Gruppo Bandello Comunicazione
Graphics: Puntoeacapo srl
Translation: Shanti Evans

ISBN-13: 978-0-7607-8882-0
ISBN-10: 0-7607-8882-0

Printed and bound in China

1 3 5 7 9 10 8 6 4 2

CHINESE ART

Filippo Salviati

Sergio Basso

BARNES & NOBLE

NEW YORK

TABLE OF CONTENTS

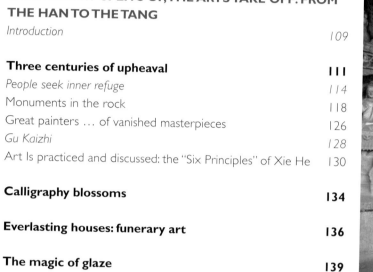

TABLE OF CONTENTS

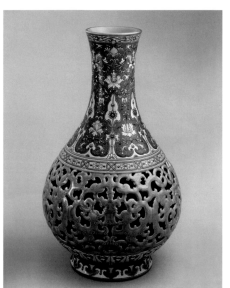

Introduction
Six Thousand Years of Chinese Art

We are faced with something of a paradox today: over the last few years, following China's entry into the World Trade Organization (WTO) and the consequent increasing internationalization of its culture, the West has shown growing interest in the more recent expressions of Chinese creativity, whether products of the avant-garde or simply of contemporary art. This may be due to the fact that more information is available, especially in published form, on the activities of contemporary artists than on their predecessors or on the traditional Chinese art that still exerts a strong influence, even on today's generation.

This book therefore constitutes the first attempt for many years to provide an introduction to classical Chinese art, albeit in a necessarily concise form that cannot hope to do justice to the complexity of an artistic tradition that is thousands of years old, but which nevertheless seeks to highlight its most salient and typical features. To put things in perspective, it is worth remembering that for the Chinese, painting and calligraphy have been considered the most important arts since at least the 4th-5th century CE. The true artist – the *wenren*, the literary man – was the one who showed himself to be well-versed and talented in the difficult arts of the brush and who was ready to devote himself, without hope of financial gain, to daily practice aimed at learning the styles and modes of expression of recognized masters of the past. In so doing he would eventually develop an artistic idiom of his own, reflecting his own individuality and the culture that had shaped him. All other art forms, from pottery to metalwork, from the carving of jade to the weaving of textiles, from sculpture to the minor or applied arts (lacquer, *cloisonné* and others), have always been the province of highly skilled but anonymous and often illiterate

1. Facing page: White and blue vase, porcelain, Ming dynasty, reign of emperor Wanli, 1573-1619. Bath, Museum of East Asian Art.

2. Dragon-shaped pendant, jade, Zhou dynasty, period of the Warring States, about 500 BCE. Toronto, Royal Ontario Museum.

craftsmen. As a result, there were no figures in classical Chinese art who were comparable with the complete Western artists of say the Renaissance, when an artist might have been sculptor and painter, architect and furniture designer, an expert in several artistic media. Another important factor distinguishing Chinese art from that of the West is its essentially private nature, or at least its restriction to circulation among a small group of individuals. It retained this characteristic until the modern era when, under the ideological impetus of Maoism, the basic principles of artistic practice were brought into question in an effort to make it more accessible and useful to the people. It is a debate that is still ongoing and one that has implications for the work of contemporary artists. This rather esoteric aspect, the fact that Chinese art was reserved for just one social class and was appreciated within only a narrow circle of practitioners and connoisseurs, has meant that, right from the outset, the art has been highly symbolic in character, a trait that pervaded it from Neolithic times until the end of the 19th century. Chinese artists became exponents *par excellence* in the art of communicating by means of images, creating a visual language that would ensure art remained the preserve of the select few who knew how to grasp the meaning behind the images. As for the artistic expressions that comprise the so-called material culture, archeology, brought to China by Western scholars at the beginning of the last century, has made a fundamental contribution

3

4

14

3. Bronze lamp with polychrome traces of a duck, found in 1987 at Wuxingzhuang, Xiangfen, Western Han dynasty, 206 BCE-8 CE. Taiyuan, Shaanxi Provincial Museum.

4. Emperor Huizong (r. 1100-1125), *Court ladies preparing newly woven*, detail, beginning of 12th century. Boston, Museum of Fine Arts.

to our understanding. Our knowledge of Chinese art from the Neolithic period through to the most recent dynasties, has been increased enormously by the information produced by archeological investigations, especially since excavations resumed on a wide scale after the relative lull that coincided with the Cultural Revolution (1966-76). However, even during that time, a number of chance but fundamental discoveries were made, such as the princely tombs in Mancheng (Lingshan, Hebei province, about 113 BCE) and the tomb of the marquise of Dai at Mawangdui (Changsha, Hunan province, 2nd century BCE). Where once scholars could only study ancient Chinese art through objects housed in European and American museums, today our understanding and interpretation of the country's artistic and cultural history are based chiefly on finds made in supervised excavations. In addition, a number of factors have helped to make us familiar with a large number of works to which it was previously hard to gain access – the creation of a modern Chinese museum network, China's inclusion in the international scientific arena, and the many exhibitions held in Western countries over the last thirty years featuring objects excavated in China or on loan from its museums. Finally, the exponential and unprecedented growth in the international market for ancient Chinese art, the publication of numerous catalogs of hitherto unknown public and private collections and the setting up of complete departments devoted to Chinese art in museums worldwide have led to ongoing reevaluation and interpretation, analyses of artistic phenomena and attributions of individual works. The study of Chinese art is endlessly absorbing and we hope that the reader will be able to share our enthusiasm for the investigation of this fascinating subject. *(F. S.)*

5

6

5. Embroidered cloth, first half of 17th century. Florence, Museo degli Argenti.

6. Feminine statue, painted wood, from burial n. 1 of Mawangdui, Changsha (Hunan province), about 168 BCE, Western Han period,

206 BCE- 8 CE. Changsha, Hunan Provincial Museum.

1. Origins: Ritual Art in the Neolithic and Bronze Ages

The long stretch of time from the Late Neolithic (about 3000-2000 BCE) to the height of the Bronze Age (about 2000-1000 BCE) can rightly be regarded as the formative phase of Chinese civilization. During this period such characteristic elements as the script, social organization and ancestor worship developed, and shape and techniques were perfected for working the materials in which Chinese creativity found its clearest expression: jade, bronze, lacquer, silk and pottery. Overall, the art of these ancient cultures can be defined as essentially ritual, an expression of religious beliefs and a symbolic, even magical and sacred manifestation of the power of members of the elite, as demonstrated by the jade objects produced by Late Neolithic cultures and the ritual bronzes of the Shang dynasty. Artistic production was more varied during the period of the Eastern Zhou, partly as a consequence of the country's political fragmentation: art had now become an expression of the wealth and magnificence of the individual courts while the variety of forms, materials and decorative themes anticipated the great artistic flowering of the later Han dynasty.

1. Facing page: Pair of bronze ritual vessels of the *hu* type, Eastern Zhou dynasty, 5th century BCE.

2. Ceramic tripod in the form of an owl found at Taipingzhuang, Huaxian (Shaanxi province), Yangshao Neolithic culture, 5th-4th millennium BCE. Beijing, Museum of Chinese History.

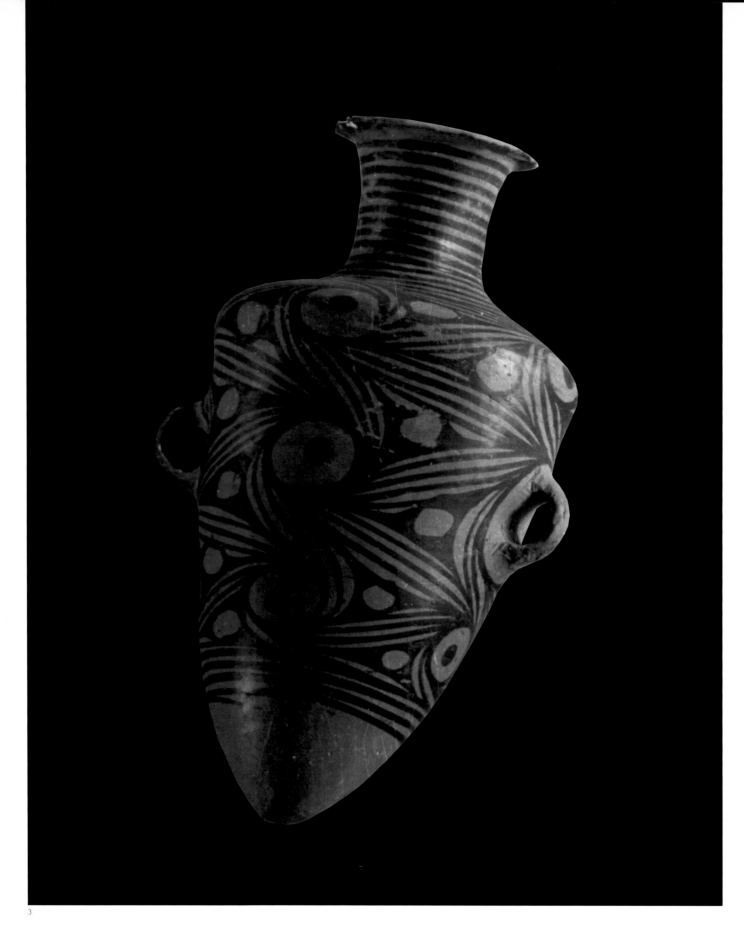

3

3. Terracotta amphora painted with geometric patterns, Yangshao Neolithic culture, Majiayao phase (Gansu province), beginning of the 3rd millennium BCE. Lanzhou, Gansu Provincial Museum.

4. Bronze buckle with
geometric decorative
motifs damascened
in gold, Eastern Zhou
dynasty, Warring States
phase, 5th-4th century
BCE, length 3.8 in (9.6
cm). Paris, Lionel Jacob
Collection, Musée National
des Arts Asiatiques-Guimet.

THE NEOLITHIC IN CHINA

For a long time most of our information on the Chinese Neolithic came from the pottery belonging to the two major cultural horizons that have been known since the early decades of the 20th century: Yangshao (c. 5000-3000 BCE), distributed over the central and north-western regions of the country and characterized by pots made from red clay and painted, and Longshan (c. 2500-1700 BCE), in which black containers thrown on the slow wheel and with incised or cut decorations are conspicuous. However, archeological discoveries of the past twenty years have made it possible to outline a more detailed picture, especially of the Chinese Late Neolithic (c. 4000-2000 BCE), a crucial phase which saw the emergence of the first stratified societies that were to develop into the states of the subsequent

Bronze Age. The now outdated "single-origin theory," which held that Chinese civilization had arisen in the middle Yellow River (Huang He) valley and spread from there to the neighboring regions, has been abandoned, following the discovery of centers of cultural diffusion in areas once regarded as marginal to those of Central China.

Moreover, some of these cultures have revealed, especially in the composition of their grave goods, an advanced level of social stratification that went hand in hand with the production of jade artifacts reserved for the elite and decorated with symbolic figures undoubtedly related to the religious sphere. The large quantity of jades found on the sites of these cultures has also made it possible to push back the date of the large-scale working of this material, one of the most characteristic of the Chinese artistic civilization as a whole, to pre— and proto-historic times.

5

5. Terracotta bowl painted with geometric patterns, Yangshao Neolithic culture, Miaodigou phase (Henan province), second half of the 4th millennium BCE. Paris, Lionel Jacob Collection, Musée National des Arts Asiatiques-Guimet.

6. Terracotta *pan* basin decorated with the motif of a snake found in a grave at the Taosi site, Xiangfen (Shanxi province), Longshan culture, about 2500-1900 BCE. Beijing, Chinese Academy of Social Sciences, Institute of Archeology.

JADE

From a strictly mineralogical perspective, the term "jade" (*yu* in Chinese) is used for just two gemstones, nephrite and jadeite. Nephrite belongs to the tremolite-actinolite series of calcium-bearing amphiboles, while jadeite is a pyroxene containing sodium. In China, the mineral nephrite was always used for jade objects : the gemstone jadeite was not worked until the 18th century, when it began to be imported from Burma. Nephrite was also known as *zhen yu*, "true jade," an honorific term that distinguished it from all similar minerals on the basis of its intrinsic properties: the quality of the stone and its color, both of which are confirmed by mineralogical studies. One of nephrite's characteristics is its density, making it one of the hardest stones to work: it is still not clear what techniques and tools were used to make the highly refined objects produced by the Late Neolithic cultures described above.

No other civilization in the world has given jade the extended importance it had in China. In the Late Neolithic period and the Bronze Age jade was used in the manufacture of ritual objects; later it was appreciated not only for its aesthetic qualities, but also for the intrinsic properties it was believed to possess. The alchemists of the Han period (206 BCE-220 CE), for example, held that jade had the power to preserve the body from decay, which explains the widespread use of jade funerary articles in the burials of the time. Even today, jade objects are among the personal talismans most prized by the Chinese people.

7

7. Grave no. 12 of the Fanshan site, Liangzhu Late Neolithic culture, 2500 BCE. Hangzhou, Provincial Institute of Cultural Relics and Archaeology. The photo shows the rich grave goods, consisting of weapons, ornaments and ritual objects, all made of jade. At top left the jade object of the *cong* type reproduced in the following picture.

8-9. Facing page: Jade ritual object of the *cong* type, found in 1986 in grave no. 12 of the Fanshan site (Yuhang, Zhejiang province), illustrated in the last picture, Liangzhu Late Neolithic culture, 2500 BCE, height 3.5 in (8.8 cm), width 6.9 in (17.6 cm), Hangzhou, Provincial Institute of Cultural Relics and Archaeology, and jade disk of the bi type, Late Neolithic period, Early Bronze Age, about 2500-1900 BCE. London, Christie's Auction House.

12

13

14

12. Dark green jade
pendant in the abstract
form of a "cloud,"
Hongshan Neolithic
culture, about 3500-2500
BCE. Tianjin, Tianjin Art
Museum.

13. Jade disk of the
bi type with relief
decoration of small
spirals, 4th-3rd century
BCE. Taipei, National
Palace Museum.

14. Jade ritual disk of the
bi type, Liangzhu Late
Neolithic culture, about
2300 BCE, diameter 8.9 in
(22.5 cm). Bonn, Private
collection.

tige and authority, decorated with images related to worship and religion in which it is also possible to discern decorative themes and motifs typical of the later Bronze Age. Among the principal cultures that display these characteristics are those of Hongshan (c. 3500-2500 BCE) and Liangzhu (c. 3300-2200 BCE), which flowered in the northeastern province of Liaoning and Inner Mongolia and in the southern Lake Tai area (Zhejiang and Jiangsu provinces) respectively.

The Hongshan culture is characterized by a considerable output of clay objects, including anthropomorphic votive images in terracotta, figurines – often of women with bulging abdomens – and fragments of life-size statues found in probable centers of worship, such as Niuheliang (Liaoning province).

The production of jade is characterized instead by ornaments carved into abstract "cloud" shapes and zoomorphic pendants in the shape of mysterious serpent-like creatures with a ring-shaped body and monstrous features: Chinese scholars recognize these last images as one of the earliest manifestations of the motif of the dragon, an iconography that was to attain its finished form under the Han dynasty. In the Liangzhu culture – which has also yielded the earliest evidence of the knowledge and working of lacquer and silk – it is apparent that jade artifacts were a clear marker of social and religious status. While the graves of ordinary individuals are located not far from their dwellings and contain few objects, chiefly stone artifacts and pottery showing traces of wear, those of members of the elite have been found far from towns and villages, set inside artificial mounds or on the tops of hills, with the graves often laid out in a regular pattern near raised structures of packed earth that were used for ritual purposes, probably as altars for ancestor worship. Jade objects found in graves can be divided into different

15

15. Jade pendant decorated in light relief, Liangzhu Neolithic culture, about 2500 BCE. Paris, Myrna Myers Collection.

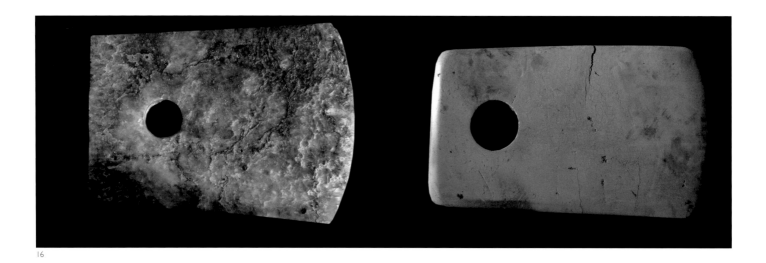

16. Pair of jade ax heads, Liangzhu Late Neolithic culture, about 2500 BCE, height 7.7 in (19.5 cm). Paris, Myrna Myers Collection. The ax on the left displays a diffuse alteration or calcification of the stone as seen in numerous artifacts of the Liangzhu culture, probably the result of exposing the objects to a powerful source of heat, such as a bonfire, following ritual acts accompanying the burial of high-ranking people.

17. Jade ritual ornament, from grave no. 16 of the Fanshan site (Yuhang, Zhejiang province), Liangzhu Late Neolithic culture, about 2500 BCE, height 2 in (5.2 cm). Hangzhou, Provincial Institute of Cultural Relics and Archaeology. The decoration, in fretwork, centers on an animal face with indistinct features, emblem of this culture.

types: personal ornaments (necklaces, bracelets, pendants), weapons (mostly axes, showing no signs of use and probably emblems of authority) and ritual objects. Among the latter, two types stand out in particular, the *bi* and the *cong*. *Bi* are disks with a hole in the middle, a polished surface and no decoration; the *cong* are parallelepipeds (three-dimensional figures like a cube, except that the faces are not squares but parallelograms) of variable height with a cylindrical hole running all the way through, and decorated with designs carved inside regular divisions on the outside and at the corners.

The actual function and symbolic value of these two objects is unknown, although references to them in writings from the later Zhou dynasty indicate they were associated with the worship of heaven and earth, which, according to the Chinese cosmological tradition, are respectively circular and square in shape. From the iconographic viewpoint, the decorative motifs carved on the Liangzhu jades can essentially be reduced to a stylized face with vague features that in the "complex version," of the kind to be seen on the jades uncovered at the sites of Yaoshan and Fanshan (Zhejiang province), becomes an anthropomorphic figure wearing a large feathered headdress set above a zoomorphic being. The frequency with which this decorative motif, perhaps an image of the main Liangzhu deity, recurs on jades of this culture makes it the characteristic stylistic feature of the related artistic production.

18

18. Jade ritual object of the *cong* type (reproduced on p. 23, fig. 8), found in 1986 in grave no. 12 of the Fanshan site (Yuhang, Zhejiang province), detail of the image carved on **four sides, Liangzhu Late Neolithic culture, 2500 BCE, height 0.8 in (2 cm). Hangzhou, Provincial Institute of Cultural Relics and Archaeology. The image represents an** **anthropomorphic being with a wide feathered headdress set above a fantastic animal.**

THE SHANG AND THE BRONZE AGE

On the basis of archeological finds, the beginning of the Bronze Age in China can be dated to around 2000 BCE, corresponding, from a historical point of view, to the period of the *Sandai* or Three Dynasties: Xia, Shang and Zhou. While Western historians are still reluctant – in the absence of reliable epigraphic evidence – to accept the existence of the Xia dynasty (traditional dates, 2205-1766 BCE), Chinese scholars tend to identify it with the Early Bronze Age finds made at Erlitou (Yanshi district, Henan province). This is an urban site where the

remains of palatial structures and tombs with bronze containers and metal plaques decorated with zoomorphic figures in inlaid turquoise attest to the presence of an elite and already stratified society, ruled, according to Chinese tradition, by the first sovereigns of antiquity. The most prominent of these was Yu the Great, reputed founder of the Xia dynasty. On the other hand, no doubts persist about the subsequent Shang dynasty (16th-11th century BCE), to which one of the first great successes of the emerging science of Chinese archeology relates: at the beginning of the 20th century the last of the capitals of this dynasty was discovered at the site of Yinxu (Henan province).

19

20

19. Bronze *jue* tripod with traces of gold leaf and lacquer, Erlitou culture (Henan province), about 1700-1500 BCE. Bath, Museum of East Asian Art.

20. Bronze plaque inlaid with turquoise dating from the Early Bronze Age, Erlitou culture (Henan province), 1700-1500 BCE, height 5.9 in (15 cm). Kyoto, Miho Museum.

21. Facing page: Bronze drum found in 1977 at Chongyang (Hubei province), decorated with the image of the taotie, a mythical creature made up of the parts of several animals, mid-Shang period, 15th-14th century BCE. Hubei Wuhan, Provincial Museum.

Amidst the remains of what appeared to be an extensive urban center large quantities of so-called "oracle bones" were discovered. These were bovine shoulder blades and turtle shells on which the Shang scribes meticulously recorded questions that the king addressed to the gods or, more often, his ancestors, on subjects ranging from matters of state, such as wars, to the yields of harvests, a crucial factor in an agricultural society like that of the Chinese. This form of divination, known as scapulamancy, has enabled us to identify the oldest form of writing practiced in China – from which derive the ideograms, or characters, still used today – and to place the Shang dynasty in its correct historical perspective, since the names of the kings inscribed on the oracle bones to a large extent match those handed down by later sources. This divinatory system was closely connected with the ancestor cult that was and still is the most widespread form of indigenous religion practiced in China at all levels of society. Closely associated with this ancestor worship are the artifacts that exemplify the art of the Shang period better than any others: the ritual bronzes, vessels of various forms used in the preparation, cooking and consumption of the food and drink presented as offerings to the ancestors during religious ceremonies. These objects indicate the central role food has always played in classical Chinese culture as an element of social cohesion; they reveal the Shang craftsmen's sophisticated knowledge of metallurgy, and display in all its force the iconography of this period, centering – as with some Late Neolithic cultures – on the theme of the "mask" or face that completely dominates the surface of the bronzes. This is the motif known as *taotie*, a mythical being made up of the parts of more than one animal whose face is characterized, especially in the bronzes of the final Shang phase, by staring eyes that protrude from the surface of the artifacts.

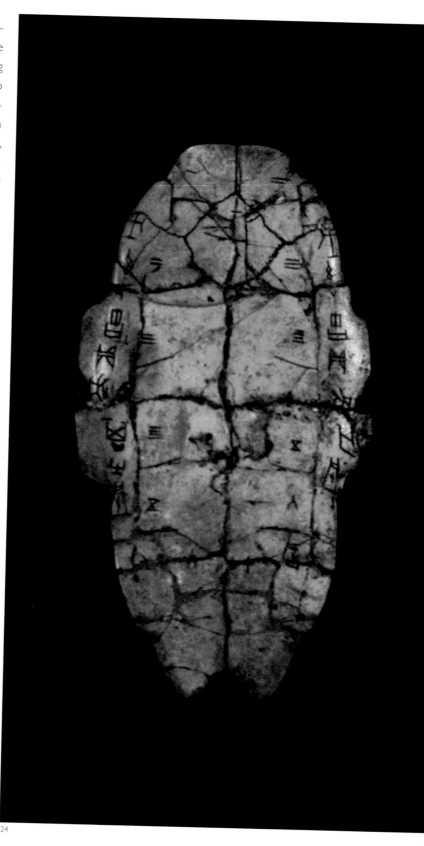

22. Facing page: *Yan* ritual vessel decorated with the *taotie* motif, late Shang-early Western Zhou dynasty, about 10th-9th century BCE.

23. Diagram of the *taotie* motif, a recurrent decorative element in the bronzes and art of the Shang dynasty.

24. Turtle plastron (breastplate) with oracular inscriptions, Shang dynasty, Anyang phase (Henan province), 13th-11th century BCE,

length 7.1 in (18 cm), width 3.9 in (10 cm). Beijing, Museum of Chinese History.

25

25. Bronze ritual vessel of the *fangding* type found at a site in South China, final phase of the Shang period, 12th-11th century BCE. Jiangxi, Jiangxi Provincial Museum.

34

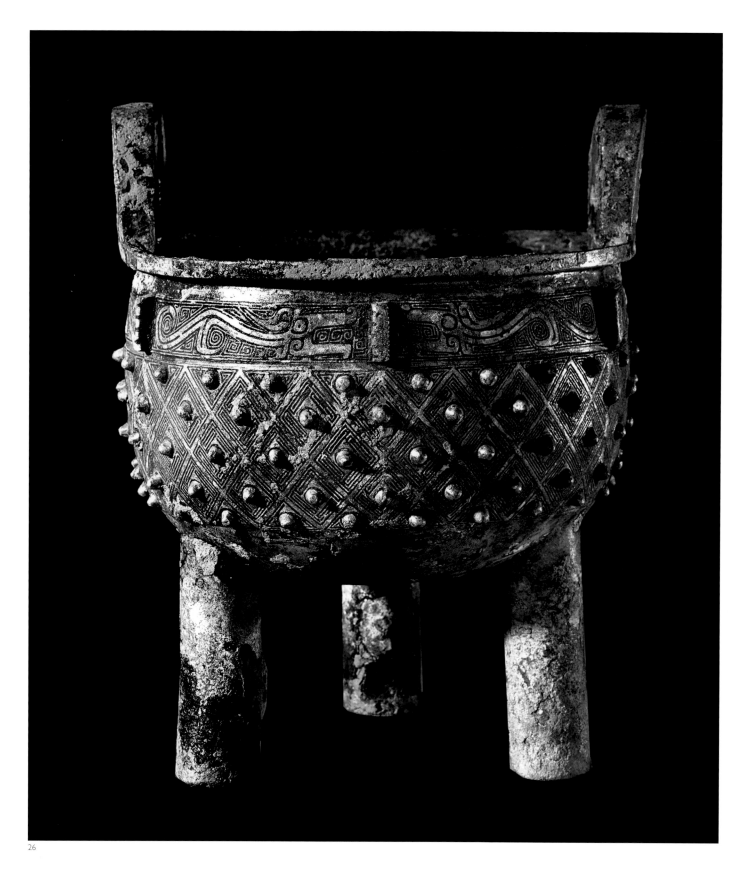

26

**26. Bronze ritual vessel
known as a *li* and used
to cook food, final phase
of the Shang dynasty,
13th-11th century BCE.
London, British Museum.**

RITUAL BRONZE OF THE YOU TYPE USED AS A CONTAINER FOR LIQUIDS
end of the Shang period, 12th century BCE
height: 12.9 in (32.8 cm)
Shanghai, Shanghai Museum

This type of bronze vessel was probably used to hold the alcoholic drinks made of fermented cereals that were offered to the ancestors in ceremonies held in their honor, or consumed by participants in the ritual. The name *you*, widely used to denote this type of container, derives from the terminology coined by students of the Song period but does not occur in contemporary inscriptions: the one on this example, made up of three characters, is thought to identify a member of the Zhu clan, an important branch of the Shang lineage, as the object's original owner.

The decoration illustrates well the stylistic features adopted during the late Shang phase in the ornamentation of ritual bronzes: on the central portion of the body is set a *taotie* mask with large, slightly protruding eyes and ears, and horns whose tips stand out strongly from the surface.

The *taotie* mask, a zoomorphic creature with indistinct features, at once an expression of Shang
religious beliefs and of their authority, also appears
on the lid, while the narrow bands around the
vessel's lip and lid are decorated with images of
dragons viewed in profile.

The prominent
protuberances or
flanges on the body
of the object mark
the points of junc-
tion of the terracotta
matrices that were
formed around the
clay model of the
object, before the
molten metal was
poured into the
mold.

The accentuation of the flanges is deliberate and seems to cor-
respond to an aesthetic tendency that emerged toward the end of
the Shang period and continued under the following dynasty of the
Western Zhou, as seen in many other bronzes of the period. The
flanges also help to delimit the compartments in which the decoration is set, thereby increasing the effect of symmetry and balance
that is stylistically characteristic of Shang iconography.

Bronze of the *lei* type used as a container for liquids, Shang dynasty.

Shang archeology has made remarkable progress since the discoveries made at the beginning of the last century, above all with the identification of the intermediate phases of this culture's development, represented by the sites of Erligang at Zhengzhou (Henan, c. 1500 BCE) and Panlongcheng (Huangpi, Hubei, c. 1500-1400 BCE).
These finds have also made it possible to establish a more accurate division of the periods in the evolution of the art of bronze: the stylistic subdivision based on analysis of the decorative motifs,

proposed by distinguished scholars some time ago, has been considerably revised on the basis of the finds made in supervised excavations. In this respect, the discovery made at Anyang in 1976 was of great significance: the only inviolate royal tomb, identified as that of Fu Hao (c. 1250 BCE), one of the consorts of King Wu Ding, which has yielded hundreds of ritual bronzes and thousands of jade objects, suggesting that the queen, ahead of her time, was a collector of artifacts made from this material. At the end of the 1980s two chance discoveries opened up further unexpected prospects of research for the archeology and art history of the late Shang period,

28

29

CHINESE ART

27. Facing page: Jade statuette in full relief, representing a kneeling woman characterized by a complicated hairstyle and a conspicuous knot in her girdle, part of the grave goods of Queen Fu Hao at Anyang (Henan province), final phase of the Shang dynasty, 1200 BCE. Beijing, Institute of Archeology, Chinese Academy of Social Sciences.

28. Jade handle of ritual utensil, mid-Shang period, 15th-14th century BCE. Bath, Museum of East Asian Art.

29. Jade bracelet, mid-Shang period, 15th-14th century BCE. Bath, Museum of East Asian Art.

demonstrating above all the extension of this culture to hitherto unsuspected areas or its influence on them.

At sites in Southern China, Xingan (Dayangzhou, Jiangxi province) and Sanxingdui (Guanghan, Sichuan province), where the presence of advanced cultural aspects contemporary with the Shang suggests nothing beyond the existing hypothesis, a huge tomb with rich contents and two sacrificial pits were respectively discovered. Both sites have yielded a large number of bronze artifacts, clearly locally produced, whose marked stylistic features differentiate them from previously known Shang bronzes, in particular for the emphasis on objects typologically different from the more customary ritual bronzes. This is well illustrated by the finds at Sanxingdui, where recent excavations indicate the presence of a large urban center and an advanced local culture. From Sanxingdui come several large bronze masks, ranging in height between 16-32 in (40-80 cm), or even more, and representing anthropomorphic faces with peculiar

30

31

30. Ivory container carved from an elephant tusk with engraved decoration and turquoise inlays, part of the grave goods of Queen Fu Hao at Anyang (Henan province), final phase of the Shang dynasty, about 1200 BCE, height 11.9 in (30.3 cm). Beijing, Institute of Archeology, Chinese Academy of Social Sciences.

31. Bronze ritual vessel for alcoholic drinks of the *fangjia* type, with inscription inside, Shang dynasty, Anyang phase, 13th-12th century, height 12.2 in (31 cm). Paris, Musée National des Arts Asiatiques-Guimet.

CHINESE ART

32. Bronze sculpture representing a fantastic being, found in 1986 at Sanxingdui, Guanghan district (Sichuan province), late Shang dynasty-early Western Zhou dynasty, 1200-1000 BCE, height 32.5 in (82.6 cm). Sichuan Chengdu, Institute of Cultural Relics and Archaeology.

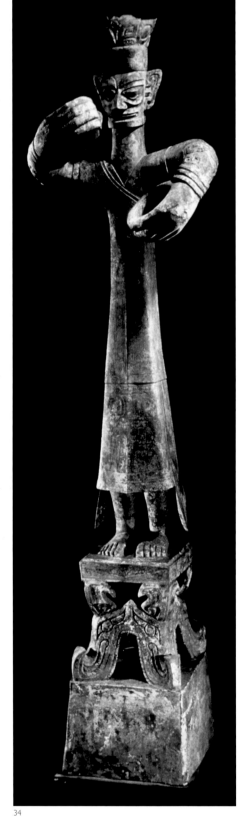

33

34

33. Bronze sculpture
in the form of a man's
head with a mask
emphasized by applied
gold leaf, found in 1986
at Sanxingdui, Guanghan
district (Sichuan

province), late Shang
dynasty-early Western
Zhou dynasty, 1200-1000
BCE, height 19.1 on (48.5
cm). Chengdu, Sichuan
Institute of Cultural Relics
and Archaeology.

34. Bronze sculpture
perhaps representing a
priest, found in 1986 at
Sanxingdui, Guanghan
district (Sichuan
province), late Shang
dynasty-early

Western Zhou dynasty,
1200-1000 BCE, height
103 in (262 cm). Chengdu,
Sichuan Institute of
Cultural Relics and
Archaeology.

features, such as enormous protruding eyeballs or pointed ears, disproportionately elongated on the outside. The perforations at the sides of these objects suggest that the masks, perhaps images of gods or local spirits, were originally fixed to wooden supports, in the manner of totems. Another discovery made at Sanxingdui is exceptional: a bronze statue over 8 ft (262 cm) high, representing a man standing on a pedestal, in a hieratic attitude, with his hands raised in front of his chest to hold a now-vanished object. It is probably the image of a priest and, in addition to its undoubted iconographic interest, constitutes tangible evidence for the advanced technological development of this local culture, contemporary with the late Shang phase and still not identified precisely. It is to be hoped that the studies currently underway and further archeological finds will be able to throw more light on the matter.

35

36

35. Bronze ritual vessel of the *liding* type used to cook food, Shang dynasty, 14th-11th century BCE, height 14.2 in (36 cm). Paris, Musée National des Arts Asiatiques-Guimet.

36. Bronze beaker of the *gu* type for alcoholic drinks, Shang dynasty, 14th-11th century BCE, height 12.6 in (32 cm). Paris, Musée National des Arts Asiatiques-Guimet.

THE PERIOD OF THE WESTERN ZHOU

The Shang kings ruled over a vast territory in which different peoples and ethnic groups coexisted, as has always been characteristic of China. These peoples – some of whom are known to us from inscriptions on oracle bones – had been subjugated by force by the Shang rulers or by their loyal servants and allies who were linked to them by ties of blood and the payment of tributes. One of them, the Zhou, who lived in Central China, along the course of the Wei River (one of the main tributaries of the Yellow River), was responsible for the first, bloody change of dynasty in Chinese history, destined to become a recurrent event in the following centuries. Around 1100 BCE the Zhou forces, led by their king Wen, attacked the Shang king in his capital Anyang and deposed him, placing a new dynasty on the throne and giving rise to what has been called "Chinese feudalism." In fact, in order to rule such a vast area, the Zhou subdivided it into administrative units governed by trustworthy vassals or by members of the royal family. The latter was based in the capital, in the vicinity of the modern city of Xian in Central China, a site whose geographical position made it the central seat of power for numerous later dynasties. Once again many of the changes that occurred in the Chinese society of the time are documented by the ritual bronzes that continued the Shang tradition of metalworking, with inscriptions added that make them precious sources of information. From such epigraphic evidence, supplementing the already substantial corpus of literary works handed down to us by this dynasty (some of the fundamental texts of ancient Chinese literature date from the Zhou period), we learn, for example, that the principal deity of the Zhou was no longer Shang Di, the Supreme Ancestor of the previous dynasty, but Tian, Heaven, and that it was Heaven which conferred on the virtuous ruler the *tian ming*, the Mandate of Heaven, with which he could govern the people. This was a political doctrine that remained the cornerstone of Chinese dynastic history up until the revolution of 1911. From a strictly artistic perspective the Zhou production of bronzes displays an initial tendency to follow the Shang tradition, but with the gradual abandonment, and eventual total disappearance, of the vessels – such

37

38

37. Bronze mask representing a fantastic being used as an ornament for a horse, Western Zhou dynasty, 10th-9th century BCE, height 9 in (23 cm). Paris, **Lionel Jacob Collection, Musée National des Arts Asiatiques-Guimet.** **38. Bronze ritual vessel of the *ding* type used to cook food, Western Zhou dynasty, mid-9th century BCE, height 8.2 in (20.8 cm). Shanghai, Shanghai Museum.**

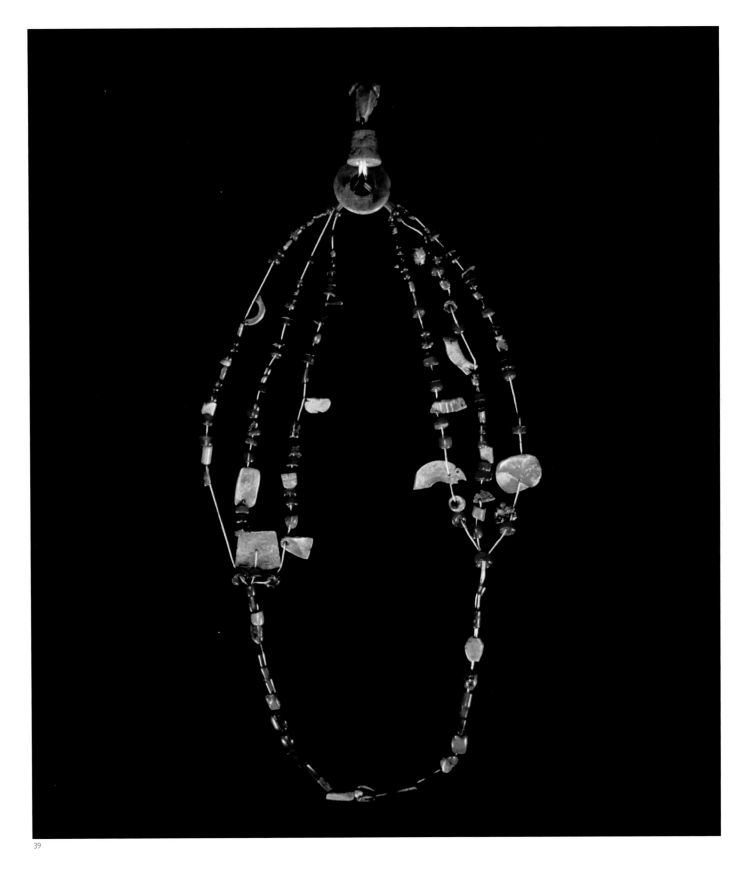

39. Composite pectoral made up of pieces of jade, agate and turquoise, found in 1984 in a tomb at the site of Liulihe, Fangshan district, in the vicinity of Beijing, early Western Zhou dynasty, about 950-900 BCE, overall length about 18.5 in (47 cm). Beijing, Central Cultural Relics Bureau.

as the *jue* cup supported on three legs or the *gu* beakers – used for alcoholic drinks made by the fermentation of cereals. According to some Zhou historians, such drinks were abused by the Shang to the point of earning them the revocation of their mandate to rule. Even the dominant motif of the *taotie* gradually lost the expressive force it had under the Shang, no doubt partly as a result of the change in religious ideas, until it was supplanted, in the final phase of the Western Zhou, by the motif of birds with large tail feathers. Over time, a different use of ritual bronzes can be discerned: while with the Shang they played a crucial part in the relations between the living and their ancestors, among the Zhou these artifacts were honorific gifts to consolidate ties of vassalage between the king and his subordinates, as can be evinced from the numerous and often lengthy inscriptions commemorating the circumstances that led to the casting of the bronze.

40

40. Bronze vase in the form of a duck, Western Zhou dynasty, 10th-9th century BCE. Henan Zhengzhou, Provincial Institute of Cultural Relics and Archaeology.

41. Facing page: Bronze vessel of the *hu* type, excavated in 1976 at the site of Zhuangbaicun, Fufeng (Shaanxi province), dated by an inscription to the reign of King Xiao of the Western Zhou, 9th century BCE. Xian, Shaanxi Provincial Museum.

THE EASTERN ZHOU AND THE "WARRING STATES"

The administrative system of the kingdom adopted by the Zhou proved, over time, a dangerous, double-edged sword. In fact, when an incursion of nomadic peoples into the heart of Chinese territory in 771 BCE resulted in the sack of the Zhou capital, the killing of the sovereign, Youwang (who had ruled from 781 to 771), and the consequent move of the capital to the east, near modern Luoyang, it became clear to the vassals that the Zhou king was losing control of his realm. Their political authority was seriously undermined by this bloody episode – the first in a series of "barbarian invasions" that China was to undergo over the course of its history – and the vassals were quick to distance themselves from the central power, strengthening their control over the territories to the point where they became independent kingdoms, with their own army, currency, administration, system of weights and measures and even script. From the artistic and cultural point of view this political fragmentation rep-

resented one of China's most intense moments of creativity, which was undoubtedly also favored by the fact that the various courts vied with one another in magnificence and wealth, as well as on the military plane. In fact the growing autonomy of individual feudal states led to the escalation of armed conflicts, not just due to the expansion of their respective spheres of influence but also because, in the period known as the era of the "Warring States" (475-221 BCE), there was open competition for who would succeed the now dethroned Zhou kings as rulers of the entire country. Over the past thirty years the discovery of inviolate tombs of members of the aristocracy of the various states has revealed the wealth and the profusion of luxury objects with which the courts of the time liked to surround themselves. They contained sumptuous embroidered silks, preserved in the tombs of Southern China thanks to the special climatic conditions; lacquered and painted objects, from bowls for everyday use to sarcophagi decorated with images inspired by the world of the dead; complicated jade ornaments, often consisting of pectorals made up of hundreds of ele-

43

42. Facing page: ceramic bell, Eastern Zhou dynasty. Eugene Fuller Seattle, Memorial Collection, Seattle Art Museum.

43. Jade pendant in the form of a dragon, Eastern Zhou dynasty, 4th-3rd century BCE. Paris, Myrna Myers Collection.

ments; metal vessels that translated the bronze repertory of previous centuries into new forms; personal ornaments like belt buckles inlaid with gold, silver, turquoise and agate that were not merely practical objects but luxurious status symbols. Apart from individual cases, however, all this "local archeology" should be set in a broader context in order to grasp a salient aspect of Chinese civilization as a whole, a civilization that has for too long been regarded as "monolithic." The archeological finds are in fact making it possible — something that the study of the history of the arts in ancient China can no longer ignore — to paint an increasingly detailed picture of the artistic development of individual provinces or cultural areas, starting from the roots of the phenomena themselves, from their earliest manifestation in the Neolithic period, and following them in time so as to identify those elements that flowed into and remained part of Chinese art in the wider sense. It is a process that clearly demonstrates the indisputable underlying multi-ethnicity of the Chinese world that, while stronger at the beginning, during the long formation period that stretched from

the Neolithic to the creation of the first centralized empire in the 3rd century BCE, persisted in a more subdued fashion throughout the history of the country, including the history of its art. This multi-ethnic character would resurface more strongly during those phases of fragmentation, of internal disunity, that alternated regularly with the periods known by the name of the ruling dynasty: Han (206 BCE-220 CE), Tang (618-907), Song (960-1279), Yuan (1279-1368), Ming (1368-1644) and Qing (1644-1911). To what we might call this internal dialectic was added interaction with different cultures and civilizations, whether nearby, like the nomadic and semi-nomadic peoples of Inner Asia, or remote, like the worlds of classical Europe, the Near East and India, echoes of whose cultures made their way into the Chinese artistic tradition thanks to the progressive intensification of trade, largely along the so-called Silk Road. In these cases the contribution of the archeology of exchange has been fundamental to the clarification of a whole series of phenomena that could be defined as "artistic contamination."

44

45

44. Belt buckle in gilded bronze inlaid with pieces of jade and glass, Eastern Zhou dynasty, period of the Warring States, 5th-4th century BCE. Private collection.

45. Bronze lamp in the form of a tree found in 1974 in the tomb of King Cuo of the state of Zhongshan, Pingshan (Hebei province), period of the Warring States, 4th century BCE.

Shijiazhuang, Hebei Provincial Cultural Relics Institute.

46. Facing page: Bronze support for drum in the form of a mythological animal, a bird with antlers, found in 1978 in the tomb of Marquis Yi of the kingdom of Zeng at

Leigudun (Hubei province), period of the Warring States, 5th century BCE. Wuhan, Hubei Provincial Museum.

The historical period of the Warring States remains the earliest in which these two different but complementary processes of exchange, useful to an understanding of Chinese art in its entirety, have been outlined with clarity. Thanks to the discovery of numerous intact noble tombs, regional archeology has made a decisive contribution to the delineation of artistic currents and to the study of individual classes of artifacts, funeral practices and religious beliefs that found one of their best means of expression in art. The graves of members of the aristocracy of the state of Jin (formed toward the end of the Western Zhou period) excavated in 1993 at Beizhao (Quwo, Shanxi, 9th-8th century BCE) are characterized by a profusion of jade ornaments: intricate pectorals in which the bodies of the deceased were clothed and true funerary masks that covered their faces, made up of numerous differently shaped elements sewn onto a piece of cloth. The northern location of the state of Jin meant that it was open, like much

of the province of Shanxi throughout its history, to long-range contacts, attested by the use of particular gemstones (such as agate and cornelian), and to possible cultural influences of foreign, Central Asian origin. At the same time, the use of large quantities of jade in funerary contexts, to cover almost the whole of the deceased's body, seems to anticipate the tradition of the jade shrouds found in princely tombs of the Han dynasty a few centuries later. Also in Northern China, the discovery of the tomb of King Cuo of the state of Zhongshan at Pingshan (Hebei, late 4th century BCE) clearly illustrates — literally, since a detailed plan of the funerary complex has been found engraved on a bronze plate — the gradual evolution of tombs into genuine forms of palatial funerary architecture. Some of the objects found in the grave, in particular mythical animals in damascened bronze, reflect the undoubted stylistic influence of the animalistic art of the steppes. In another geographical context, what used to be generically called the

47

48

52

47. Sculpture in painted wood representing a stag, Chu culture, period of the Warring States, 5th century BCE. Paris, Musée National des Arts Asiatiques-Guimet.

48. Bronze basin containing a *zun* vessel for alcoholic drinks decorated with an intricate ornamentation of serpentine creatures, from the tomb of Marquis Yi of the state of Zeng found at Leigudun (Hubei province), 5th century BCE. Wuhan, Hubei Provincial Museum.

49

50

49. Set of bronze bells mounted on lacquered wooden stands (modern), from the tomb of Marquis Yi of the state of Zeng found at Leigudun (Hubei province), 5th century BCE. Wuhan, Hubei Provincial Museum.

50. Lacquered wooden sarcophagus painted with fantastic zoomorphic creatures, from a tomb found at Baoshan, Jingmen (Hubei province), second half of 4th century BCE, length 72.4 in (184 cm). Jingzhou (Hubei province), Jingzhou Museum.

"Huai style," a definition used for the stylistic features of Southern Chinese art (typified by the prevalence of plaited ornamental themes, a preference for animalistic figures of a mythical or monstrous character and extensive use of the techniques of damascening in bronze work), is known today to be largely an expression of the Chu culture, named after the most powerful state in South China. Over the course of its gradual political expansion, the Chu state swallowed up more than forty minor principalities, setting in motion processes of acculturation, until it became the last of the rivals of the Qin kingdom before the latter finally unified the country in 221 BCE. The princely tombs of Xiasi (Xichuan, Henan, 6th century BCE), the silk fabrics found at Mashan (Jiangling, Hubei, 4th-3rd century BCE), the lacquers and inlaid bronzes from Baoshan (Jingmen, Hubei, early 4th century BCE) and the wooden sculptures set up to guard the tombs at Tianxingguan (Jiangling, Hubei, mid-4th century BCE) are all examples of the art produced in the area under the influence of the Chu culture, together with the ritual vessels and bronze sculptures (in which the lost-wax technique was used in virtuoso fashion to produce intricate and dynamic forms) found in 1978 inside the tomb of Marquis Yi of the state of Zeng at Leigudun (Suixian, Hubei, c. 433 BCE), one of the most important discoveries in the whole archeology of the period of the Warring States. (F. S.)

51

51. Steel sword with damascened inscription in gold, from the tomb of King Guo Jian of the state of Yue, discovered at Jiangling (Hubei province), 5th century BCE, length 21.9 in (55.6 cm). Wuhan, Hubei Provincial Museum.

52

52. Lacquered wooden bowl of the *dou* type, from the tomb of Marquis Yi of the state of Zeng found at Leigudun (Hubei province), 5th century BCE, height 9.6 in (24.3 cm). Wuhan, Hubei Provincial Museum.

BRONZE BUCKLE WITH DAMASCENING IN GOLD, SILVER AND TURQUOISE

Eastern Zhou period, Warring States phase, 4th-3rd century BCE
length: 6 in (15.2 cm)
Private collection

A stupendous example of the skill attained in the working of metals in ancient China, this buckle is modeled in the shape of a tiger or dragon biting the tail of a fabulous bird, perhaps a phoenix. The theme of combat between animals is the stylistic mark of the animalistic art produced by the semi-nomadic populations which the ancient Chinese had to confront, on the military level as well, until the consolidation of the centralized empire under the Han. While the object is of Chinese manufacture, it epitomizes the cultural and artistic exchanges of the time between China and the nomadic peoples of the north.

Even the function of the artifact, a buckle used to tighten a belt, indicates the adoption by the Chinese of a garment foreign to their traditional attire: pants. These too reached China through the nomadic peoples, following the spread of horses, which not only became a symbol of noble status but were also utilized to back up the detachments of foot soldiers that made up the backbone of the armies.

Bronze buckle with damascening in the form of a tiger attacking a deer, from the tomb of King Cuo of the kingdom of Zhongshan, Eastern Zhou dynasty, Warring States phase, 4th-3rd century BCE. Hebei, Hebei Provincial Museum.

The buckle's magnificence and
size indicate the power and
wealth of its owner, undoubtedly
a member of one of the many
local aristocracies that flowered
during the period of the Warring
States, vying with one another
not only on the military plane
but also in their ostentation, as
the lavish noble tombs that have
been excavated demonstrate.

On the technical and ornamental level, the buckle shows the
advances that had been made in metalworking: the mono-
chromatism that characterized bronze artifacts created under the Shang and Zhou dynasties has given way to intense
coloristic effects made possible through the application of
metals like copper, silver and gold without heating, by insert-
ing them into cavities made in the object during its casting
in molds, often with the addition of inlays of semiprecious
stones like turquoise, here used for the eye of the tiger.

2. China Unified under the Qin Dynasty

The year 221 BCE is a fundamental date in Chinese history: it was the moment when the country, after centuries of internecine strife, was unified under a single sovereign, Qin Shi Huangdi, who has gone down in history as the "First Emperor." Owing to the pragmatism that characterized his rule and the brief duration of the dynasty he founded, not much has survived of Qin art, although one of the greatest archeological discoveries of the 20th century must be ascribed to it: the famous army of terracotta soldiers, located in the vicinity of the burial mound housing the remains of the First Emperor (Xi'an, Shaanxi province). This magnificent example of ancient Chinese statuary is characterized by an intense realism that is reflected in the faces of the clay warriors. The first section of another monument symbolic of China, the Great Wall, was also built in this period.

1. Facing page: Statue of officer, Qin dynasty, 3rd century BCE. Lintong, Xi'an (Shaanxi province), Museum of the Terracotta Statues of the Mausoleum of the First Emperor.

2. Head of warrior, Qin dynasty, 3rd century BCE. Lintong, Xi'an (Shaanxi province), Museum of the Terracotta Statues of the Mausoleum of the First Emperor.

秦始皇

姓嬴名政始目始皇乙卯即王位庚辰併天下稱皇帝
在位三十七年居王位二十五年即帝位十二年壽五十

廿

THE FLOWERING OF CHINESE PHILOSOPHICAL THOUGHT

The period of the Warring States was undoubtedly a troubled time in China's long history but it was also the most fertile in relation to the development of its thought and philosophy. Indeed, to some extent it may have been the unstable political situation – as in the city-states of ancient Greece – that stimulated reflection on human nature, on ethics and morality, on the best way of administering a state, on the natural principles that govern the world and on the "becoming of things." The "Hundred Schools of Thought" that flourished in the second half of the Zhou's reign saw the emergence of key figures like Lao-tzu (Laozi in Pinyin), probably a figure of legend and traditionally author of the classic text of Taoism, the *Tao-te Ching* (*Daodejing*, "The Book of the Way and Its Virtue"), and Confucius (Kongfuzi, c. 551–479 BCE), who laid the doctrinal foundations on which the thinkers of the following

4

3. Facing page: Imaginary portrait of Qin Shi Huangdi, the First Emperor, about 1900. London, British Library.

4. Watercolor painting of Lao-tzu on his buffalo followed by a disciple, 18th century. Paris, Bibliothèque Nationale.

5. Three-armed bronze lamp in the form of an immortal (*xian*) with wings and a body covered with feathers, Western Han dynasty, 2nd-1st century BCE, height 14.2 in (36 cm). Private collection. The three arms terminate in dragon heads.

centuries were to hone their wits. The Taoists preached renunciation of the world and a return to the simplicity of the natural order of things, which human beings had to follow, like the current of a river, in order to find the Tao, the Way, bringing their own existence into harmony with that of the world. Confucius's thought had a more markedly political character and focused on the principles needed to reestablish the order of things and relations within a society torn by civil wars, lacking a common system of ethics that could act as a cohesive force to reinforce the ties between all the members of the human community. However, the school of thought that struck the deepest chord at the courts of the time, which were regularly visited by thinkers in search of a "sponsor" for their teachings, with the result that they came to be known as "wandering philosophers," was that of the Legalists, or the School of the Law (*Fajia*), whose main exponent was Shang Yang (sometimes called Wei Yang, first half of 4th century BCE). The school of the Legalists was founded on a solid *Realpolitik*, which taught that human beings were inherently selfish and that this made necessary

an organized state ruled by a powerful sovereign and governed by strict laws. Appointed prime minister by Duke Xiao of Qin, Shang Yang was given the chance to put into practice what he preached in the work *Shang Jun Shu* ("Book of the Lord of Shang"). He completely reorganized the kingdom on the basis of the drastic Legalist principles, which held that agriculture and war constituted the foundation of a stable state, not the practice and study of literature, history, philosophy and art, which would eventually corrupt and weaken the character of the people and their rulers. Thanks to the adoption of this ideology and the reorganization of the army into a formidable machine of war and death, technologically superior to that of other states in that its soldiers were equipped with iron rather than bronze weapons, Qin embarked on its inexorable conquest, which reached a triumphal conclusion in 221 BCE when the last opposing kingdom, Chu, was defeated and China was finally unified after centuries of division under the rule of a single sovereign: Qin Shi Huangdi, otherwise known as the First Emperor, founder of the Qin dynasty (221–206 BCE).

6

7

6. Imaginary portrait of the philosopher Confucius, 17th century. Paris, Bibliothèque Nationale.

7. Sandstone stele representing Lao-tzu next to the Jade Emperor, Northern Wei dynasty, 527 CE, 10.9x10.8 in (27.8x27.5 cm). Beijing, Museum of Chinese History. Lao-tzu was deified and venerated as a god from the 2nd century CE on: here he is shown seated alongside the Jade Emperor, the god who presides over the large religious pantheon worshiped by the Chinese people.

THE TERRACOTTA ARMY AND THE MAUSOLEUM OF THE FIRST EMPEROR

Accounts of the strength and ferocity of the Qin military forces were handed down for centuries by Chinese literary sources. Then, in the summer of 1974, the chance finding of a terracotta statue of an ancient soldier by some farmers led to what turned out to be one of the most important archeological discoveries of the 20th century: the terracotta army of soldiers posted to guard the eternal sleep of Qin Shi Huangdi. The army constitutes just one part, although the most spectacular, of the imposing funerary compound that the First Emperor had erected to ensure that posterity would remember him and his work. The mausoleum is situated to the east of Xian (Shaanxi province), on the plain traversed by the Wei River, which runs to the north of the compound, and is bounded to the south by some heights, one of which, Mount Li, gives its name to the whole archeological complex, known as the "necropolis of Mount Li." Commenced in 246 BCE, the year of the ascent of Prince Zheng, the future First Emperor, to the throne of the state of Qin, the mausoleum was still unfinished

when he died in 210 BCE. This was partly due to the enormous size of the compound which covers an area of over 22 square miles (56 square kilometers) centered on the tomb of Qin Shi Huangdi, a mound that is now only 166 ft (50.5 m) high but originally reached a height of nearly 500 ft (150 m). Inside was found the inviolate burial chamber housing the remains of the ancient ruler. The mound is located in an eccentric position, inside two rectangular sets of walls built out of pressed earth, outside and around which sacrificial pits have been uncovered containing the remains of human and animals victims immolated at the time of the First Emperor's death, as well as funerary objects such as terracotta statuettes of kneeling men and women. In addition, the foundations of various buildings and underground drainage channels have been found in the northern part of the funerary compound. These are the remains of a group of palaces, watchtowers and temples for the worship of ancestors that are mentioned in historical sources and once formed the complex of architectural structures associated with the burial mound. They were constructed by tens of thousands of conscripts and artisans, who must also have been engaged in making the clay statues of the soldiers.

8

8. View of the burial
mound marking the
site of the tomb of Qin
Shi Huangdi, the First
Emperor, 3rd century BCE.
Lintong, Xi'an.

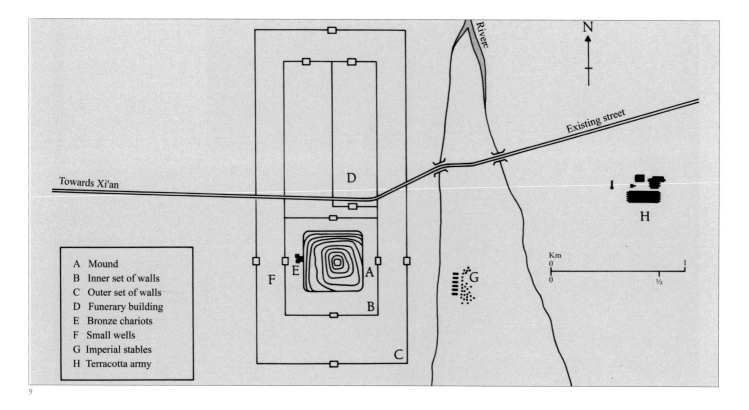

N

Rivere

Existing street

Towards Xi'an

D

Km
0   1
0   ½

H

F   E   A

G

B

C

A   Mound
B   Inner set of walls
C   Outer set of walls
D   Funerary building
E   Bronze chariots
F   Small wells
G   Imperial stables
H   Terracotta army

9

10

**9. Plan of the
archeological complex of
the mausoleum of Qin Shi
Huangdi, 3rd century BCE.
Lintong, Xi'an.**

**10. Funeral stele marking
the beginning of the avenue
leading to the tomb of the
First Emperor, 3rd century
BCE. Lintong, Xi'an.**

11. Statue of charioteer, detail of the bust, Qin dynasty, 3rd century BCE. Lintong, Xi'an.

12. Facing page: Statue of a foot soldier, Qin dynasty, 3rd century BCE. Lintong, Xi'an.

hesitated to kill soldiers who disobeyed or showed cowardice at the moment of attack. The clay generals who commanded the army of the First Emperor were discovered in pit no. 3, excavated between March and December of 1977. This is a chamber of irregular shape which contained a war chariot and sixty-eight statues with an average height of 6 ft 3 in (1.9 m), many of them representing officers. The soldiers that accompany them, probably their personal guard, are wearing both light and heavy uniforms. The daunting appearance, the facial features and expressions of the officers, like those of each of the thousands of terracotta figures, are vividly depicted, genuine individual portraits, each modeled separately. It is said that the aim was to represent the many different ethnic groups in the China of the day, for the first time united under the command of a single man; but it is likely that portraying each soldier individually was intended to "bring to life" the army that had the task of accompanying and protecting the sovereign in the world of the dead.

Apart from this surprising and celebrated peculiarity of the terracotta army, a degree of standardization necessary for the realization of a work on such a vast scale can be seen in the handling of the figures' bodies. The lower part is solid while the torso is hollow, as is the head, which was set in the hole between the shoulders and held in position by a long neck. The heads, made in molds, were individually finished to bring out details like the features of the face, ears, moustache and hair. Modeled separately, the forearms and hands were intended to hold the weapons with which the soldiers were originally equipped, but these were later removed by rebels, who also destroyed the pits by setting fire to them. One of the measures taken by Qin Shi Huangdi immediately after the unification of China, in fact, was the confiscation of all the arms in the country, so that the only armed force was that of the imperial army. However, the move, made in part to discourage potential insurrections, did not prevent the popular uprising that led to the fall of the Qin dynasty, placing on the imperial throne Liu Bang,

18

CHINESE ART

17. Facing page: Statue of an archer, detail of the head, Qin dynasty, 3rd century BCE. Lintong, Xi'an.

18. Statues of foot solders of the terracotta army, Qin dynasty, 3rd century BCE. Lintong, Xi'an.

19-20. Following pages: Statue of a soldier, detail of the head and statue of an officer with a pleated skirt, Qin dynasty, 3rd century BCE. Lintong, Xi'an.

THE GREAT WALL

The building of the Great Wall is traditionally ascribed to the First Emperor, who is said to have ordered its construction to defend the northern borders of China, where there were few natural barriers, from incursions by the nomad peoples of the North, which had caused the military and political downfall of the Zhou dynasty. Study of written sources and information derived from archeological investigations, however, indicates that Qin Shi Huangdi had in reality ordered the restoration, consolidation and linking up of existing stretches of defensive walls erected by the rulers of the northern kingdoms of Qi, Wei, Yan and Zhao, later conquered by Qin. The fortifications constructed on the express orders of the First Emperor are thought to have been confined to an even smaller area, limited to the region of the Ordos, the territory bounded by the great bend traced by the Yellow River in Central China as it makes its slow descent to the sea. A passage in the *Shiji* ("Historical Records"), compiled by the historian Sima Qian (145-90 BCE) of the succeeding Han dynasty (206 BCE-220 CE), tells us that Qin Shi Huangdi commanded his general Meng Tian to drive the nomadic groups back across the Yellow River. Once this had been accomplished a series of fortifications – or fortified citadels, depending on the interpretation – were erected to prevent future incursions. In fact historical documents ascribed to this dynasty do not mention the building of such an imposing defensive structure, which suggests, considering the pragmatism typical of the Qin kingdom, that the "great work" was not a priority in the government's program. The costly maintenance of the Great Wall (known in Chinese as the "10 000-Li Long Wall") was largely neglected by the rulers of later dynasties, up until the reconstruction carried out at the beginning of the Ming dynasty which gave the monument the appearance it has today. *(F. S.)*

25

**25-26. The Great Wall
of China as it has looked
since the time of its
reconstruction during
the Ming dynasty.**

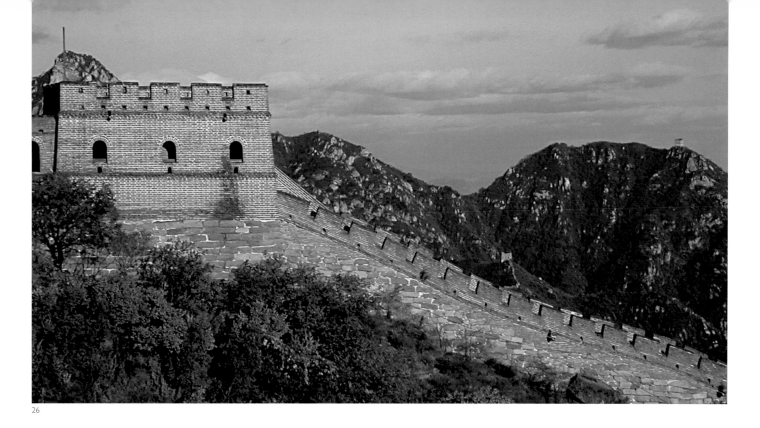

26

27

79

CHINESE ART

27. The Great Wall
of China, detail of one
of the gates.

3. Consolidation of the Empire: the Han and the Silk Road

The centralized government structure introduced with the unification of the country by the Qin was then inherited and improved upon by the Han dynasties that followed them. Hard on the heels of the consolidation of the empire came its first territorial expansion, with the annexation of part of South China and what is now Korea, and, most importantly, the extension of control over Central Asia following the military campaigns waged against the nomadic peoples called the Xiongnu. The latter was an undertaking of great significance, bringing China into contact with different countries and cultures for the first time, and officially initiating the export of silk, one of its most highly valued wares. The Buddhist faith also spread along the caravan routes and was to exercise a huge influence on Chinese art in the centuries to come. Evidence for this is mainly to be found in the rich contents of the princely tombs of the period, which make it possible to reconstruct many aspects of life and religious beliefs in the time of the Han.

1. Facing page: Silk banner illustrating the journey toward immortality in the world of the dead, from the tomb of Lady Dai at Mawangdui, Western Han dynasty, 2nd century BCE. Changsha, Provincial Museum of Hunan.

2. Incense burner in the shape of Mount Bo, the abode of the immortals (*boshanlu*), from the tomb of Prince Liu Sheng at Mancheng, Western Han dynasty, 2nd century BCE, height 10.2 in (26 cm). Wuhan, Provincial Museum of Hebei.

THE HAN DYNASTY

The Han dynasty sprang from a popular uprising – one of many to determine the succession of lineages occupying the imperial throne – led by Liu Bang, later crowned emperor with the dynastic title of Gaozu (206-195 BCE). It was one of the longest dynasties in Chinese history, lasting for over four hundred years, and only interrupted, about halfway through, by the usurpation of the throne by Wang Mang (9-25 CE). This brief interregnum was followed by the period of the Eastern Han, when the capital was moved from the original Chang'an (modern Xian) to Luoyang. It was an important period for China, not just because it saw the establishment of political and military sway over the bordering regions – resulting in one of the greatest expansions of territory in China's history – but also because it brought a gradual

consolidation of the empire: the class of state officials responsible for administrating the state emerged, while Confucianism was made the official ideology (c. 136 BCE), and the corpus of texts attributed to the philosopher or handed down by him to posterity became the foundation of the entire Chinese cultural edifice. The invention of paper (1st century BCE) favored the diffusion of written texts, whether literary works, poetical compositions or historical treatises like the monumental *Shiji* ("Historical Records") compiled by Sima Qian (145-86 BCE), founder of the great tradition of Chinese historiography. Art flourished too, but all that survives of the paintings and calligraphic works that adorned the sumptuous imperial palaces and aristocratic residences of the time is an echo in contemporary writings: the contents of the tombs give an idea of the levels of artistic production of the period and provide us with some tangible examples.

3

3. One of the imperial
tombs in the vicinity
of Xian where the
emperors of the Han
dynasty are buried.

4. Bronze statue of horse,
Eastern Han dynasty,
2nd century CE. Beijing,
Institute of Cultural
Relics.

5. Terracotta funerary
statuettes of male and
female attendants,
Western Han dynasty,
2nd century BCE. Toronto,
Royal Ontario Museum.

6. Terracotta funerary
statuette of a cook
preparing food, probably
from Sichuan province,
Han dynasty, 1st-3rd
century CE, height 11
in (28 cm). Paris, Lionel
Jacob Collection,
Musée National des Arts
Asiatiques-Guimet.

CHINESE ART

PRINCE LIU SHENG AND LADY DAI

Two noble tombs of the period shed light on certain aspects of Han art and culture. Both made for individuals of high lineage, they were discovered by chance in the 1970s, becoming "classics" of modern Chinese archeology. The first, uncovered at Mancheng (Hebei province), was the grave of Prince Liu Sheng and his consort Dou Wan, who was related to the Han ruling house. The monumental tomb, with its burial chamber and other rooms carved out of the living rock of the mountain, owes its fame to the shrouds or burial suits made from pieces of jade in which the mortal remains of the two aristocrats had been dressed., As we have seen, jade was prized since the Neolithic period, and was invested with many symbolic values in the Han period. It was regarded by the alchemists as having the power to stop the decomposition of the physical body after death. This belief was responsible for the inclusion of large quantities of jade in graves and for the curious practice of clothing the entire body of deceased members of the nobility in it. Moreover, the ideas about the attainment of "immortality" that had obsessed the first Chinese emperor Qin Shi Huangdi remained popular during the Han dynasty, as shown by the many images of immortals found in the tombs of the period.

Tradition held that these immortals were custodians of the secret of longevity, which they jealously guarded on the inaccessible islands where they lived, situated in the East China Sea. The second important discovery was made in the south of China, at Mawangdui in the vicinity of the city of Changsha (Hunan province): the inviolate tomb of a noblewoman, Lady Dai, wife of the governor of Changsha. The excellent state in which the delicate artifacts that made up the rich grave goods had been preserved, despite the passing of many centuries, caused a sensation. There were lacquered wooden dishes and bowls, painted with elegant motifs in red and black and used for the preparation and consumption of food; groups of wooden funerary statuettes of musicians and attendants still with the vivid colors of their original polychromy; three wooden sarcophagi set one inside the other and painted with motifs inspired by the afterworld, populated by fabulous creatures. The most exciting discovery of all was made inside the inner sarcophagus: the body of the marquise, preserved almost intact by the thick layers of white clay and charcoal that sealed the tomb and still dressed in a total of twenty silk dresses in practically perfect condition. Draped over the sarcophagus housing the remains of Lady Dai was a banner, also made of silk and painted with scenes depicting the noblewoman's journey to the world of the dead.

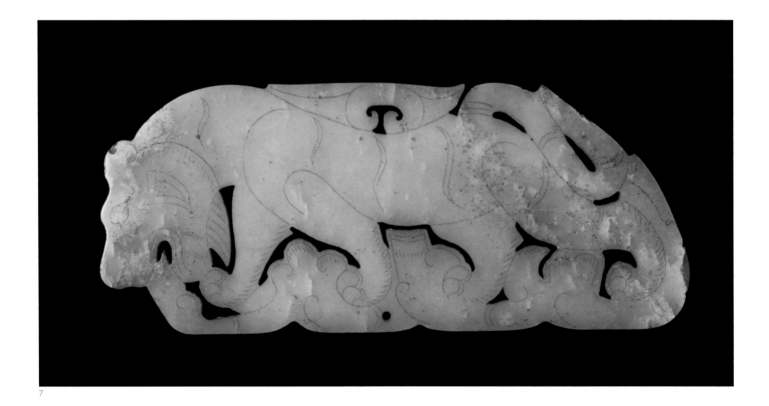

7

86

7. White jade pendant with engraved and openwork decoration representing a tiger, Western Han dynasty, 2nd-1st century BCE, length 7.5 in (19 cm).

Paris, Musée National des Arts Asiatiques-Guimet.

8. Gilded bronze lamp,
from the tomb of Princess
Dou Wan at Mancheng
(Hebei province), Han
dynasty, first half of 2nd
century BCE. Beijing,
Institute of Cultural Relics.

9

9. Bronze mirror, from
the tomb of Lady Dai at
Mawangdui, Western Han
dynasty, 2nd century BCE.
Changsha, Provincial
Museum of Hunan.

10

11

CHINESE ART

10. Lacquered containers, from the tomb of Lady Dai at Mawangdui, Western Han dynasty, 2nd century BCE. Changsha, Provincial Museum of Hunan.

11. Polychrome painted wooden statuettes of a group of musicians, from the tomb of Lady Dai at Mawangdui, Western Han dynasty, 2nd century BCE, height of the tallest 9 in (23 cm). Changsha, Provincial Museum of Hunan.

BURIAL SUIT MADE OF PIECES OF JADE THREADED TOGETHER WITH GOLD WIRE

from the tomb of Prince Liu Sheng at Mancheng (Hebei province), found in 1968
Western Han dynasty, 2nd century BCE
length: 74 in (188 cm)
Hebei, Hebei Provincial Museum

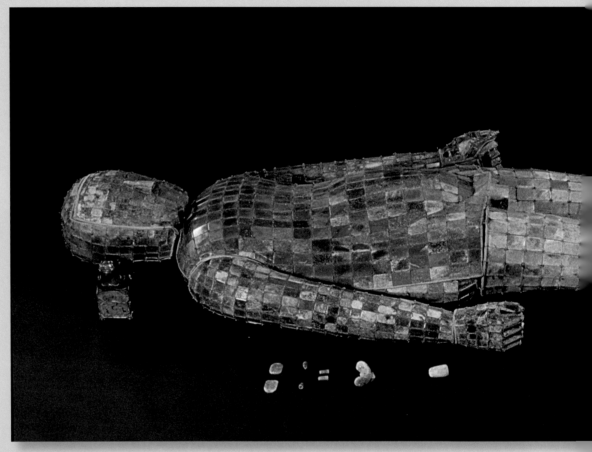

Prince Liu Sheng, who died in 113 BCE, was the son of the fifth Han emperor, Jingdi (reigned 157-141 BCE), and the brother of his successor to the throne, Wudi (reigned 141-187 BCE). The jade burial suit in which his remains were dressed is still the most famous of the more than forty examples of this extraordinary type of arti-fact discovered by archeologists, mostly at sites in Eastern China.

Suit made of pieces of jade in which Princess Dou Wan, wife of Prince Liu Sheng, was buried.

It appears that only high-ranking nobles related to the royal house could be buried in a full shroud: other aristocrats were usually entitled to use jade to cover the face, and sometimes the hands and feet too. Rank was also differentiated by the type of metal wire used to hold together the thousands of pieces of jade of which these burial suits were made up: gold, silver or copper. Liu Sheng's burial suit required a total of 2468 gold wires.

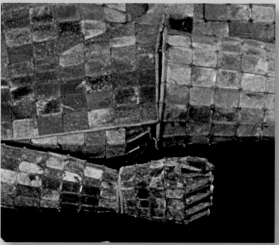

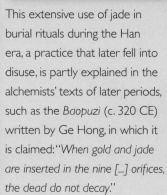

This extensive use of jade in burial rituals during the Han era, a practice that later fell into disuse, is partly explained in the alchemists' texts of later periods, such as the *Baopuzi* (c. 320 CE) written by Ge Hong, in which it is claimed: "*When gold and jade are inserted in the nine [...] orifices, the dead do not decay.*"

The Han period finds show that such beliefs and practices were widespread in China long before the 4th century CE. In fact, as well as being dressed in the jade burial suit, the nine openings of Liu Sheng's body – eyes, nostrils, ears, mouth, anus and genitals – were sealed with jade 'plugs' to prevent the qi ("essence, vital fluid") from leaving the body, resulting in decomposition. The purpose of this remains, however, a matter of pure conjecture.

SILK

China has been famous for its silk since antiquity, and the techniques used to make it were long cloaked in mystery. Tradition held that the wife of Huangdi, the mythical Yellow Emperor and legendary father of Chinese civilization said to have lived around 3000 BCE, first discovered the properties of the filament produced by silkworms of the species *Bombyx mori*, the only lepidopteran that was raised in China for the production of silk. Today, thanks to archeological finds, we have more accurate information on the origins of sericulture (cultivation of the silkworm) and these, surprisingly, turn out to be as old as the legend claims. In fact, as previously noted, the earliest silk articles discovered come from sites belonging to the Late Neolithic culture of Liangzhu. These few but significant finds provide unequivocal evidence that silk was already known to the ancient Chinese at the very time indicated by the legends about the Yellow Emperor and his consort, a period coinciding with the dates of the Liangzhu culture. In addition, these important discoveries suggest that silk-working first emerged in the southern regions of China, where the main centers of production of the precious fabric were located in the historic era: Hangzhou and the Lake Tai region and, heading up the Yangtze River (Chang Jiang) to the west, Chengdu, the capital of the southwestern province of Sichuan. Silk is a very fragile organic material that deteriorates rapidly, and is rarely found in ancient graves.

Although the records tell us that it was known and worked during the Shang and Western Zhou dynasties, burials of the subsequent period of the Warring States (475-221 BCE) provide the first tangible evidence of silk artifacts, like those discovered in the princely tombs excavated in the vicinity of Jiangling, capital – at the time of the Warring States – of the powerful kingdom of Chu, whose territory covered the whole of Southern China.

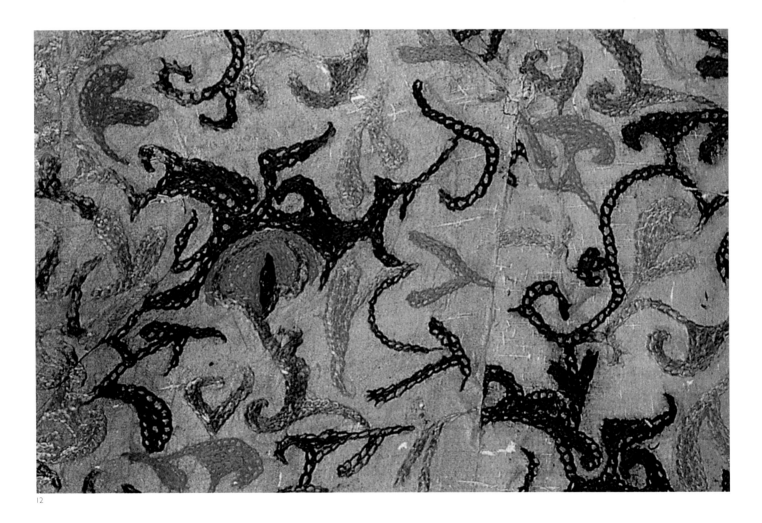

12

12. Embroidered silk, from tomb no. 1 at Mawangdui, Western Han dynasty. Changsha, Provincial Museum of Hunan.

13. Facing page: Embroidered silk, from tomb no. 1 at Mawangdui, Western Han dynasty. Changsha, Provincial Museum of Hunan.

HAN CHINA AND THE XIONGNU NOMADS

When did China start to export silk, a material prized even by the Romans, which had earned the Chinese, in Latin sources, the name "Seres"? Not before the end of the 3rd century BCE, when Han China found itself having to fight off the nomad population of the Xiongnu, who had begun to threaten the country's northern frontier in the second half of the 4th century BCE, even making raids into Chinese territory. It is a story worth telling because it induced China, for the first time, to turn its gaze on the lands of the West, discovering the existence of other countries and civilizations with which, directly or indirectly, it began to establish relations.

Around 210 BCE the Xiongnu succeeded in occupying the Ordos region, located inside the great northern bend of the Yellow River, forcing Emperor Gaozu (206-195 BCE) to come to terms. The result was that a young woman of the Chinese imperial family was given in marriage to the ruler of the Xiongnu: every year from then on, according to Chinese sources, the nomads were offered gifts of silk yarn and fabrics, fermented beverages, grain and other foodstuffs. The quantity of silk handed over to the nomads must have been large: it was not just a gift made by the Chinese emperor to the leader of the Xiongnu, but also a form of annual tribute paid to discourage the nomads from obtaining such goods for themselves by periodically sacking Chinese territory. In 175-174 BCE, the emperor Wendi (180-157 BCE) sent a letter to the Xiongnu ruler accompanied by a number of gifts, including bolts of a wide variety of silks: raw, embroidered, painted with floral motifs and in a range of colors.

It is clear that the Chinese rightly regarded silk as the rarest and most precious of their products, and therefore the best offering that could be made to win over a foreign sovereign, especially one who led the formidable nomadic peoples. However, the Chinese were also aware of the fact that the delicate silk fabrics and yarns could not have been widely used among the Xiongnu, nomads of the steppe who wore clothes made from the hides and fur of animals. In fact the Xiongnu used the silk given to them by the rulers of China as valuable merchandise to be traded with other peoples of Inner Asia, thereby facilitating the spread of the textile outside the borders of China. It was by this route, passing from hand to hand, that the precious fiber arrived first in the regions of the Near East and then in the territories under the control of Rome.

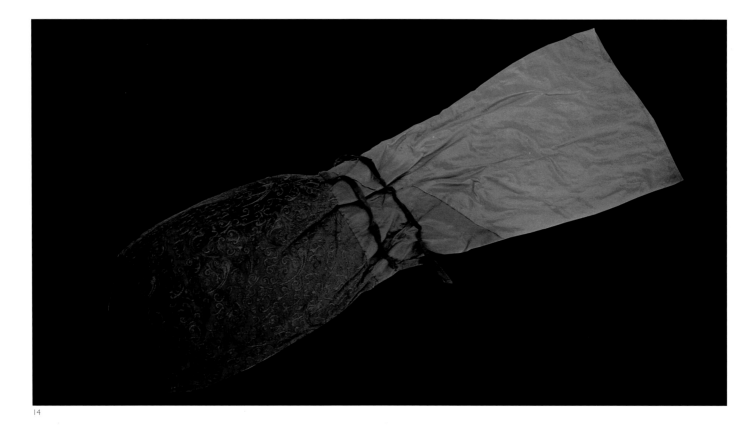

14

14. Embroidered silk pouch, from tomb no. 1 at Mawangdui, Western Han dynasty, 2nd century BCE. Changsha, Provincial Museum of Hunan.

15. Facing page: One of the polychrome terracotta statuettes found in the vicinity of the burial mound of Emperor Jingdi (reigned 157-141 BCE) of the Western Han dynasty. Xi'an, Shaanxi Provincial Archeological Institute.

THE MISSIONS OF ZHANG QIAN AND THE DISCOVERY OF THE WEST

The Chinese rulers' cautious policy of paying tribute took a different turn when the emperor Xiaowu (141-87 BCE), known by his posthumous name Wudi, came to the throne. After hesitating for a few years, he chose to change attitude toward the Xiongnu and send them, instead of delicate silk, the powerful Chinese armed forces under the command of generals who were determined to assert themselves. In 133 or 132 BCE, seeking allies in the military conflict he had launched against the nomads, Wudi sent an official called Zhang Qian on a mission to the West. After a long series of adventures, he succeeded in reaching a territory situated to the north of the Amu Darya (known in antiquity as the Oxus River), corresponding in part to the modern republics of Uzbekistan and Tajikistan. Fording the river, Zhang Qian headed south, arriving in what is now Northern Afghanistan, at the time called Bactria in classical sources and "Daxia" by Zhang Qian himself. In this region the imperial envoy made a significant discovery. With great wonder, he recognized that some of the products and textiles brought from India and sold in the markets of Daxia actually came from Yunnan and Sichuan, the two southwestern provinces of China. He immediately reported his discovery to the emperor, speculating that there must be a route linking Southwestern China with India. In fact, such a route did exist, leading to the basin of the Ganges

16

16. Polychrome terracotta statuettes of horsemen, from Yangjiawan, Western Han dynasty, 2nd century BCE, average height 26.6 in (67.5 cm). Shaanxi, Xianyang Museum.

through the mountains of Burma, still used in part today by modern smugglers. Along the road flourished a commerce controlled by no political authority, in which goods passed from hand to hand without those at either end of the clandestine trade route even knowing the origin of the merchandise they exchanged or what its final destination would be. The goods that traveled along this road in the second half of the 2nd century BCE included the silk fabrics from Sichuan seen by Zhang Qian in the markets of Bactria. When he returned home around 126 BCE, Zhang Qian drew up an official report on his adventurous journey, which he presented to the emperor. The first Chinese ever to travel to such distant places, he collected an enormous amount of information on foreign lands and peoples of which nothing had previously been known in China. As well as territories that he had visited in person, traveling through an area made up of part of the present-day states of Kazakhstan, Uzbekistan, Tajikistan and Afghanistan, the imperial envoy learned indirectly of the existence of countries like India and Parthia and the region of the Persian Gulf. From what he saw and could deduce from the accounts of others, Zhang Qian realized that neither silk nor the trees from which lacquer was made were to be found in any of the territories extending from the Fergana Valley, in Uzbekistan, to the regions controlled by the Parthians. This signaled the opening of interesting economic prospects for China, at that time the only producer of silk and lacquer.

The military policy adopted by Wudi against the Xiongnu relied on

17

**17. The burial mounds
of the Han emperors near
Xi'an (Shaanxi province).**

30. Painted terracotta oil lamp decorated with applied figurines of immortals and animals, found in 1972 at Jianxi Xilihe, near Luoyang (Henan province), end of the Eastern Han period, 2nd century BCE, height 36.2 in (92 cm). Luoyang, Institute of Cultural Relics.

31. Wall painting representing several figures, from a tomb at Luoyang, Han dynasty. Boston, Museum of Fine Arts.

4. The Court Splits Up, the Arts Take Off: from the Han to the Tang

At the beginning of the 3rd century CE, political power was in the hands of a swarm of generals. The son of one of these satraps attempted the impossible. To legitimize the situation, and inaugurated a new dynasty with its capital at Luoyang. This set off a chain reaction, with an opposing clan setting up another court at Jiangye, now modern-day Nanjing. The heirs of the ruling dynasty were obliged to retreat to the west, entrenching themselves in the peripheral region of Sichuan. After five hundred years, the unity of the empire had been shattered. It would be another 350 years before it could be united once more, nearly four centuries of internal struggle, during which time different military leaders sought to enlarge their own territories, establishing dynasties that rarely lasted more than a generation. But the presence of rival courts meant that there were more patrons and the formation of different artistic milieus, each championing an aesthetic and a taste of its own. Let us take a look at a series of fundamental events that will help us to understand the developments in the history of the period's art.

1. Facing page: Sculptures decorating cave 12, Northern Wei dynasty, about 460-94 CE. Luoyang, Longmen Caves.

2. Sculpture of the bodhisattva Padmapāṇi ("Lotus Bearer"), Northern Wei dynasty, 527 CE. Toronto, Royal Ontario Museum.

THREE CENTURIES OF UPHEAVAL

North and South China developed in distinctly different directions. In the north, already under the Han dynasty, the army had opened its ranks to ever greater contingents of barbarians. In the 4th century, non-indigenous populations not only swept into China at breathtaking speed and in vast numbers, they also seized power. The prize at stake was control of the Yellow River basin.

The dynasties that succeeded one another in the south, on the other hand, could count on control of the Yangtze River and a formidable fleet, but they were short of men. The landowners were the real rulers, forming states in their own right and not always allowing their subjects to serve in the army. The disturbances in the north induced a million peas-

ants to flee south. It was a displacement that would bring changes to various aspects of life: to diet (in the north people ate dry cereals, millet and wheat, while in the south they ate rice); to language (each immigrant community tried to maintain its own dialect, while it was in each dynasty's interest to standardize the language); to sexual relations (in the north, under the influence of nomadic traditions, women enjoyed a degree of freedom, but in the south, society was by and large polygamous). But ultimately the influx of population proved a boost to the prosperity of the south. The port of Guangzhou (Canton) established a steady trade with Southeast Asia; the word of Buddha, carried along the caravan routes for some time, now arrived by sea as well. The landowning aristocracy grew increasingly entrenched, showing a tendency to transform itself into a closed elite by blocking access to the administrative powers. To the north,

4

3. Facing page: Monumental sandstone figure of the Amitābha Buddha in cave 20, Northern Wei dynasty, about 460-93 CE. Datong, Yungang Caves.

4. The "hanging" monastery constructed on the cliff of Mount Hengshan, Northern Wei dynasty. Datong, Mount Hengshan.

in Shanxi, the Tuoba established a foothold. A nomad people in contact with Chinese culture, they displayed an impressive flexibility by embracing sinicization, adopting Chinese customs and manners in order to play a part in the balance of power in the region. In 398, under the name of the Wei dynasty, the Tuoba founded the capital of Pingcheng (today Datong) and twenty years later they conquered the traditional capital, Luoyang, moving their court there in 493. The power of the Wei was based on the effective agrarian reforms that they introduced and the adoption of Buddhism as the state religion. Every couple received a parcel of land, one part of which was used to grow mulberry or hemp, but on reaching the age of sixty the land had to be returned to the state. The taxation system, based on land, was fixed and was to last for three hundred years. When the Sui from the south eventually succeeded in unifying the country, this was the system that they inherited. In 533 the Tuoba split into two rival factions. Tiring of forsaking its own tribal traditions, a large section of the aristocracy called a rapid halt to the process of sinicization and the capital was moved to the west, to Chang'an (modern Xian). This marked the birth of the Northern Zhou. Those who wished to continue with assimilation moved to the east, to Ye; in the space of a generation they would change their name to the Northern Qi. Forty years later, in 577, the former annexed the latter, but in 581 both succumbed to the Sui, the dynasty destined to reunite the country.

5

5. Buddhist monastery,
cave no. 12, Northern Wei
dynasty, about 460-93 CE.
Datong, Yungang Caves.

6. Stone sarcophagus with engraved decoration, detail of one side showing scenes of filial piety, Northern Wei dynasty, about 525 CE. Kansas City, Nelson-Atkins Museum of Art.

PEOPLE SEEK INNER REFUGE

In the period known as "Sixteen Kingdoms and Six Dynasties" (304-589 CE), named for the dizzying pace of political change, people devoted themselves to religious speculation and a life of contemplation, seeking an inner refuge from the chaos surrounding them. This shift in thinking was led by the Taoist school, and above all by the Buddhist religion. The Taoists took part in alchemical research in an attempt to create the elixir of life from mercury, and in so doing developed an understanding of chemistry that would also prove useful in pottery and pharmacology.

They preached a return to a spontaneous relationship with nature. A famous example was the group known as the "Seven Sages of the Bamboo Grove" who, in the middle of the 3rd century, would gather together in the countryside (in this case the capital, Luoyang) where they passed the time drinking wine and discussing philosophy, traveling on a cart drawn by a stag. Their irreverent attitude toward the authorities even cost some of them their heads, as happened to Ji Kang. Denounced and condemned to death, he awaited decapitation contemplating the lengthening of the shadows while he played the lute. The appeal to immerse oneself in nature, at the heart of Taoist thought, must have had a strong influence on the renewal of landscape painting. Even in the centuries that followed, the artist roving mountains and forests with a brush in his knapsack and ready to paint whenever inspiration took him, was a constant theme. One strain of Buddhism in particular quickly gained a foothold in China.

I. Portrait of Ji Kang, from *The Seven Sages of the Bamboo Grove*, detail, Northern dynasties.

II. Relief in dark limestone with traces of color representing the empress and her retinue, from the Binyang cave (Longmen Caves), Northern Wei dynasty, about 522 CE.

Kansas City, Nelson-Atkins Museum of Art.

III. Facing page: Buddhist stele representing *The Great Journey*, Northern Wei dynasty, 523 CE. Toronto, Royal Ontario Museum.

SPECIAL FOCUS

This was the school known as Mahayana, or the Great Vehicle, which held that certain individuals, after attaining the enlightenment that will free them from the continual cycle of rebirth, choose to reenter the world to act as spiritual guides for others. A person who makes this choice is called a bodhisattva, "one whose essence is enlightenment." The earliest record of a Buddhist monastery dates from 148 CE. In the mid-4th century CE, in the heart of Central Asia, Kumarajiva, a Buddhist monk and the son of an Indian Brahmin and a princess of Khotan, was taken prisoner by a Chinese general. He learned the native tongue in prison and, when freed, set about translating the Buddhist canon from Sanskrit into Chinese. Most of the texts he translated were from the doctrine of the Great Vehicle. The Buddhist monks were skilful propagandists, they had handbooks of preaching and would readily use the language of the ordinary people. Following their example, scholars too began to use the well-known historical tales of the time in their writings, creating the oldest written stories, which were military sagas. The Tuoba dynasty used Buddhism as a powerful force for social cohesion, persuading believers that their

IV

IV. Fresco representing the paradise of Amitābha, detail, Tang dynasty. Dunhuang, Mogao Caves.

rulers were incarnations of Buddha. It was therefore in these rulers' own interests to finance the construction of the cave temples and the colossal statues of the Buddha that were in reality effigies of themselves! The Buddhist statuary and wall paintings in the temples therefore had to conform to the rules of a detailed portraiture that was at times used to immortalize the earthly features of the patriarchs of the various schools, while at others to follow the rigid iconography of the divine hierarchies.

By the 5th century monasteries had sprung up everywhere. Also functioning as hospitals, inns and banks, among other uses, they also served to concentrate land, labor and even capital in the hands of the monks. This accumulation of power threatened the Wei emperor, triggering a first wave of persecution in 445. The imperial guard found a deposit of arms and wine in one of the capital's monasteries, a threat to both the court and its customs.

As a result, Buddhism was subjected to periods of particularly violent repression, but it was not until 845 that it suffered a setback from which it never fully recovered.

V

V. *The Teachings of the Buddha,* Northern Wei dynasty, about 386-535 CE. Datong, Yungang Caves.

crossroads on the so-called "Gansu corridor" in Central Asia. This is where Chinese culture, the Central Asian culture of the oases of Turfan, Khotan and Kucha, met and interacted with Indian culture, creating new forms and artistic schools. In each case, these monumental complexes are like "open construction sites" to which new temples were added, carved out of the rock by each successive dynasty, and where it is possible to trace the evolution of style in sculpture and painting almost decade by decade. Broadly speaking, the Wei dynasty moved rapidly from a basis of colossal, solid and not very animated forms, to a marked linearity, while under the Northern Qi statues regained their solidity, but with more proportion and animation than was evident at the beginning of the Wei period.

In the case of Dunhuang, for example, the process began in the 4th century (under the northern dynasty of the Liang). A monk of Indian origin called Lezun had a vision of a procession of a thousand Buddhas passing in front of him. He decided to carve out the first cave on the spot and so began the complex of Qianfodong ("The Caves of the Thousand Buddhas").

To date the different caves, it helps to look at the range of colors used in the frescoes and the arrangement of the figures. Northern Wei figures, for example, were sharply outlined in white, giving them a more luminous appearance. Today our perception of the colors used by the artists is somewhat distorted by the oxidation of the pigments over time, with pink darkening into brown, but the rapidity of the line, the dynamism of the images and the multitude of figures that vie to fill every bit of wall, seize the imagination, opening up a whole world of stories despite the passage of many centuries.

Since the rock available at Dunhuang proved too friable for the sculptors to work, they were obliged to construct a core of mud, dung, plaster and straw. This was then covered with a layer of pure white

9

9. Statue of seated Buddha. Datong, Yungang Caves.

10. Facing page: Sculptures and wall paintings. Datong, Yungang Caves.

11
12

**11-12. Two statues
of the standing Buddha.
Qingzhou.**

clay and finally paint could be applied. Tales of the various incarnations of the Buddha Shakyamuni (the *Jātaka*) were told in lively compositions crowded with figures, which only grew more orderly under later dynasties.

Seeking a way to atone for the persecution of 445, the repentant Wei emperor was persuaded by the monk Tanya to initiate a series of cave temples, and in 460, the first statues were carved out of a sandstone cliff at the site of Yungang.

We have to imagine that the architecture was a harmonious combination of carved stone and wooden building. The wood has not survived the ravages of time; the sand-laden wind from the north, which still troubles the inhabitants of Beijing at certain times of year, has eroded the features of the statues and parched the landscape, which must have looked much more attractive then than it does today. At Yungang, a group of fifty-four caves, colossal, single, central figures predominated initially, increasing to groups of five by the 7th century (a Buddha, two disciples and two bodhisattvas). In 439, the Wei Tuoba conquered the Gansu and brought settlers in from Dunhuang by force, swelling the ranks of the craftsmen working in and around the caves.

The decoration of cave temples 9 and 10 (dating from 480; forty years after work first started) clearly takes its inspiration from the Great Vehicle of Buddhism: verandas are laid out in front of the caves, and inside, a space left around the base of the central statue allows the faithful to walk around it; two rows of paintings run along the walls, the lower illustrating stories of the Buddha's previous lives, the upper thronged with *apsaras*, celestial beings in adoration of the transcendent Buddha, Vairocana. As we lift our gaze from the lower to the upper row, we pass from an everyday vision of the Buddha as a man with a place in history, to one of a divine being beyond time.

Caves 5 and 6 reveal a first stylistic revolution and a new taste for

13

**13. Cave temples,
Northern Wei dynasty.
Longmen.**

angular, linear and slender forms; the tendency shifts from the mass to the line, to the two-dimensional, almost to the comma; the flaring of the clothes often terminates in a fishtail. At Longmen, near the new capital of Luoyang, the sculptors found themselves working with gray limestone instead of sandstone, a harder material that permitted greater detail. At the Luoyang site, 350 cave temples were carved out of the rock until the 8th century, with only a few later additions. The Guyang (495) and Binyang (first quarter of the 6th century) caves are good examples. There is the same division into rows of images, portraying scenes from the Buddha's previous lives into which figures containing the portraits of the frescoes' patrons are inserted; the ceiling is decorated with an immense lotus blossom. The statuary decoration is composed of three triads. The colossal figures still demonstrate a fondness for solidity, precision and mass that has not yet diverged from the style of Yungang: the

shape of a truncated cone can be recognized in the neck, a cylinder in the bust, and a cube in the head. It is only in the smaller Buddhas and the Binyang cave that we can detect a tendancy to reduce bulk and slim down the figure. Another stylistic change took place in the second half of the 6th century, under the Qi dynasty, at the site of Xiangtangshan, between Henan and Hebei, again in the vicinity of a Wei capital, in this case Ye. This was prompted by the change in the material available. The stone used in the caves near Ye came from quarries of white micaceous marble, which permitted great precision of detail and was ideally suited to the bright colors and gilded outlines that the Wei sculptors liked to use. Here the statues acquire a new solidity, and the heavy drape of their clothes is evident. Could this renewed taste for mass have been due to the influence of the Indian Gupta canon, which had reached China by sea through Southeast Asia?

14

14. Fengxian Temple, detail, Tang dynasty. Longmen.

15. Facing page: Cave of the Ten Thousand Buddhas, interior, Tang dynasty, 680 CE. Luoyang, Longmen Caves. At the center the Buddha Amitabha surrounded by the monk Ananda, the bodhisattva Káśyapa and guardians. On the ceiling, a lotus blossom.

GREAT PAINTERS ... OF VANISHED MASTERPIECES

While the northern dynasties distinguished themselves as patrons of Buddhist rock art, the southern court of Nanjing played host to many painters. All the works painted on silk have been lost, but the theoretical discussions of the 4th century have survived, revealing the tastes of an elite whose concern was to reclaim nature by reproducing it. In the salons of the capital, the *fu*, a literary form praising landscapes, was very popular, and private gardens were much in vogue. Painting also followed this fashion, often illustrating the themes of pastoral poetry rather than portraying the landscape directly.

The courtiers seem to have embarked on an "artificial incorporation" of nature, through the creation of a microcosm in reaction to the surrounding chaos.

Zong Bing, in his *Hua shanshui xu* ("Introduction to Landscape Painting"), stressed the advantages of contact with nature through painting rather than direct experience: in a painting the *qi*, the "vital force," of an enormous mountain can be concentrated in just a few square inches, and a resonance can be established between the hearts of the viewer and the painter. It is no coincidence that the concepts of concentrating nature's vital force in artistic works and of heart "speaking" to heart

are Buddhist in origin. The almost monochrome image of a painted landscape is preserved on the wall of one tomb. Given the funerary context, this landscape seems to allude to a view of the life to come, rather than to represent a scene from a past existence. However, the majority of the decorated tiles found in various tombs depict – as in the Han period – genre scenes, not necessarily pastoral, in which the figures are enjoying the everyday pleasures of food, fellowship among students, the company of friends or a trip into the countryside. The artists depict the cooking utensils, fashionable hairstyles, toys and board games of the time with obsessive precision.

A pair of funerary statuettes (*mingqi*) shows two officials working together on endorsing the archives: one holds the records for the other, who is busy with the brush. The Chinese of this era who were contemplating the approach of death wished to stress their attachment to the small things in life and to the values of solidarity: immortalizing the warmth of a contact, the sharing of a small joy, the sadness of a memory that was perhaps already unbearably distant in life.

In a tomb at Xishanqiao, near Nanjing, one wall is decorated with the "Seven Sages of the Bamboo Grove." For the artist the theme of the seven sages had the advantage of reconciling the fascination with nature with conviviality. We have no knowledge of the original works of the painters, but historians have handed down their names and admiring artists of later generations made copies of their masterpieces. The problem is that, while the Chinese tradition of copying the painters of the past was an invaluable means of learning, artists often liked the challenge of taking inspiration from an ancient composition and pitting their skill against its creator in an effort to improve on it. So we need to exercise a degree of caution when faced with the copy of a work, as we do not know the extent to which the original theme has been reworked.

Take the case of Gu Kaizhi, a genius of the 4th century. Two copies of one of his paintings exist. Are we justified in thinking that the two different scrolls can help us to reconstruct Gu's original composition more faithfully? Not at all, given that the later of the copies was made seven hundred years after Gu Kaizhi's death, and that both versions may have been executed in turn from other copies, and not directly from the original.

In the specific case of Gu Kaizhi, the aspect which raises most suspicion is that – if we are to believe the copies – right up until the 13th century, the themes of Chinese painting had been tackled and resolved in the work of a single man. It is much more likely that the artists who took their inspiration from Gu introduced later elements into their copies.

16

16. Wall painting representing a landscape in the tomb of Prince Ruru, Eastern Wei dynasty.

17. Funerary statuette
in terracotta (*mingqi*)
representing a pair
of officials endorsing
records, Western Jin
dynasty.

Gu Kaizhi was born around 345 at Wuxi, in Jiangsu, under the Jin dynasty. He went on to become the secretary of Grand Marshal Xuan Wen. We know that he painted pictures in color with the outlines traced in ink. He was famous for his religious murals (he had the idea of making pilgrims pay to see them as a form of self-financing for the building of a monastery), and his portraits. He would translate famous poems into images as an exercise and it was this kind of painting that the landscap-

ists of later dynasties liked to copy. The *Admonitions of the Court Instructress* (*Nü shi zhen*) is an illustration of a poem by Zhang Hua (232-300). The landscape articulates the figures in space, where they are placed side by side. Their arrangement in the space is only slightly more "cunning" than in the lacquered wooden screen found in the tomb of Sima Jinlong (an important figure in the Jin dynasty), dating from 484.

The *Nymph of the Luo River* (*Luoshen fu tu juan*) illustrates a poem by Cao Zhi, written in 222. Two versions of Gu Kaizhi's painting have come down to us, one of them – in the Museum of the Imperial Palace, Beijing – in a much more archaic style than the other, now housed in the Freer Gallery in Washington.

In *Luoshen fu tu juan*, the landscape already serves to link the figures in a fluid way, a much more mature solution than in *Nü shi zhen*. Birds fly from one episode to the next, guiding the reading of the work; the gaze of the figures is used in a similar way to help us to understand what is happening.

Finally, we have a particularly interesting literary source of information on Gu Kaizhi, the *Hua yuntaishan ji* ("On Painting the Cloud Terrace Mountain"), in which the painter himself describes the solutions he adopted when painting the mountain of the title. The picture was a portrait of the circle of the Taoist Zhang Daoling, set in a burgeoning nature. Here the relationship between man and landscape has changed drastically, and seems to be that of a painter of the 10th century.

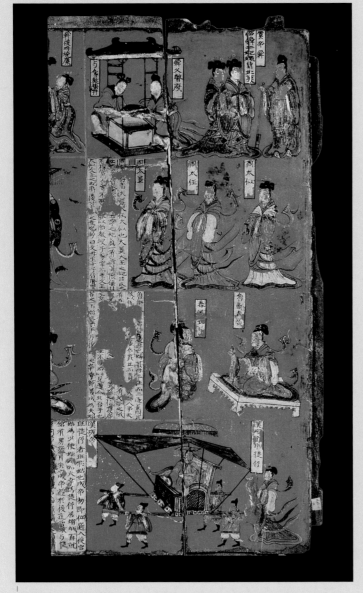

I

III

I. Panel with lacquered painting on wood, from the tomb of Sima Jinlong, 190.9x15 in (484.8x38 cm). Datong, Civic Museum.

II. Gu Kaizhi, *The Admonitions of the Court Instructress* (*Nü shi zhen*), copy from the Tang period, detail. London, British Museum.

III. Gu Kaizhi, *The Nymph of the Luo River* (*Luoshen fu tu juan*), copy from the Song period, detail, 8.5x225.5 in (21.7x572.8 cm). Beijing, Palace Museum.

20

21

20. Fresco representing
devas listening to the
teachings of the Buddha,
from cave 272, period
of the Six Dynasties.
Dunhuang, Mogao Caves.

21. Fresco representing
The Prince and the Tigers,
from cave 428, period
of the Six Dynasties,
about 557-81 CE.
Dunhuang, Mogao Caves.

EVERLASTING HOUSES: FUNERARY ART

Surprisingly, the spread of Buddhism had little effect on the funerary art of the aristocracy. The elite were not cremated, and the architecture of their tombs, along with their rituals, did not differ greatly from that of the Han tradition. No imperial mausoleums have yet been found, only a few tombs of princes, guarded by pairs of huge stone animals forming avenues leading to the place of burial, the *shen dao*: *qilin* (unicorn) and *bixie* (a sort of chimera) or lions facing one another are examples of colossal statuary and represent awesome power, but are nevertheless cold, inert, and immobile. In the south, the majority of tombs are rectangular in plan and have tunnel vaults fronted by a long, narrow antechamber. The walls of these antechambers are decorated with everyday subjects of the kind that were already dominant in the Han period, such as a procession of officials, but are now accompanied by both Buddhist images (like the *apsaras*, celestial beings celebrating the Buddha) and Taoist themes, such as the "Seven Sages of the Bamboo Grove;" celestial images are reserved for the ceiling. The tombs were still

26

27

26. Silver gilt goblet found at Datong, Northern Wei dynasty, 4th century CE. Shaanxi, Provincial Museum.

27. Miniature temple carved from limestone for oblations, Northern Wei dynasty, about 527 CE. Boston, Museum of Fine Arts.

CALLIGRAPHY BLOSSOMS

The number of Chinese characters is staggering (there are up to 64,000 written characters), but in reality they combine just eight basic strokes. These are the ones children study at elementary school and the great calligraphers practice unceasingly. Over the course of its thousands of years of history, the Chinese system of writing has developed several different styles: *lishu*, or the clerical script, once in vogue among officials and now used solely for ceremonial purposes; *kaishu*, the sober, elegant and slender script that is the standard for publishing; *xingshu*, or "running" script, employed for private uses such as diaries and notes; *caoshu*, or "grass" script, a kind of cursive writing in which the strokes dissolve into mere graphic and at times incomprehensible hints at characters, an expression of the calligrapher's uncompromising originality. The script was written from right to left, and from top to bottom; each character had to be composed and balanced within an imaginary square, and the various characters in a column were supposed in turn to suggest a mutual equilibrium. Wei Heng, who died in 291, compiled a history of the four styles of writing. His daughter, Lady Wei Shuo (272-349), taught calligraphy to Wang Xizhi (303-361). With uncommon chivalry, Chinese tradition gives a woman the credit for having trained one of the most refined artists of the Middle Kingdom. In fact Wang, along with his son, Wang Xianzhi, who

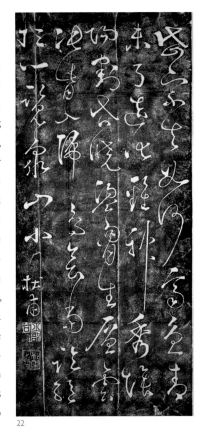

22

SEAL

RUNNING

CURSIVE

WILD CURSIVE

SIMPLIFIED

23

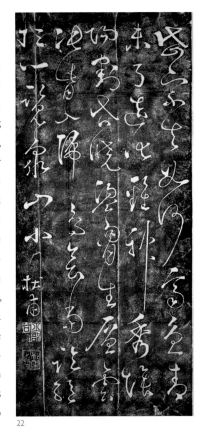

24

22. Example of calligraphy from the Tang period. Xi'an, Shaanxi Provincial Museum.

23. Examples of calligraphic styles, in order: seal, running, cursive, wild cursive and simplified (in use since the 1950s to encourage literacy). **The character used for the examples, *xiě*, means "to write."**

24. "*Preface to the Poems Composed at the Orchid Pavilion*" (*Lanting xu, Shenlong ben* version), copy of a calligraphic work by Wang Xizhi (303?-361 CE), *xingshu* **calligraphic style. Beijing, Palace Museum.**

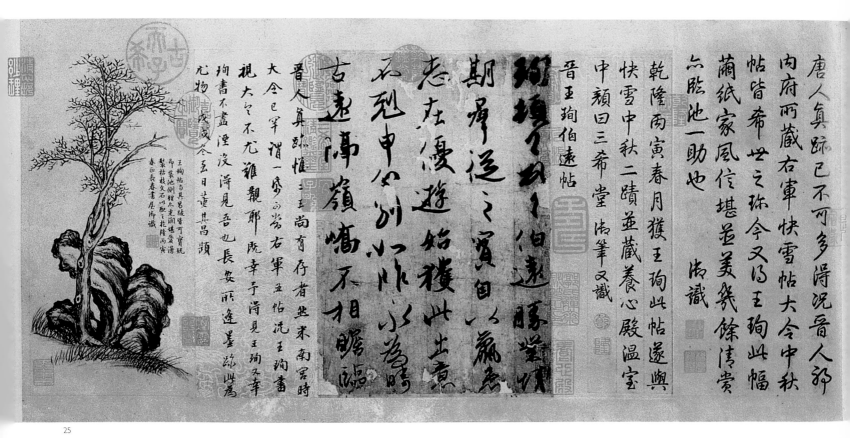

was also his pupil, would be regarded in the Tang period as the greatest calligrapher ever to have lived. Unfortunately nothing has survived of his work, or that of his son, as the emperor Taizong decided to take Wang's masterpieces with him to his tomb. So to get an idea of Wang's art we have to make do with a fragment by Wang Xun, Wang Xizhi's nephew and pupil. It consists of just five lines of a letter to a friend, telling him that he has no time to pay a visit, yet they are sufficient for us to grasp the calligrapher's ability to create a dynamic tension, thanks to the alternation of characters written with great force with others left in a more fragile state. When painting or working on a piece of calligraphy the Chinese artist assumes a special posture. The legs are spread to the same width as the shoulders, the elbow never rests on the table and the brush is held at right angles to the scroll, so that the wrist is free to transfer the mental image of the subject directly onto the paper or silk. In this way, the line made on the surface of the scroll indicates the position of the master's wrist precisely, making it possible, even at a distance of centuries, for an aspiring modern calligrapher to imitate the writing of a great artist of the past. By following the path taken by the original artist's hand as if it were the choreography for a dance, the modern calligrapher can also imagine the movements of the wrist that generated that script.

25. Wang Xun (350-401 CE), *"Letter to Bo Yuan"* **(*Bo Yuan tie*), cursive *xingshu* calligraphic style, 9.9x6.8 in (25.1x17.2 cm). Beijing,** Palace Museum. The original section consists of the five central columns, on a darker ground.

EVERLASTING HOUSES: FUNERARY ART

Surprisingly, the spread of Buddhism had little effect on the funerary art of the aristocracy. The elite were not cremated, and the architecture of their tombs, along with their rituals, did not differ greatly from that of the Han tradition. No imperial mausoleums have yet been found, only a few tombs of princes, guarded by pairs of huge stone animals forming avenues leading to the place of burial, the *shen dao*: *qilin* (unicorn) and *bixie* (a sort of chimera) or lions facing one another are examples of colossal statuary and represent awesome power, but are nevertheless cold, inert, and immobile. In the south, the majority of tombs are rectangular in plan and have tunnel vaults fronted by a long, narrow antechamber. The walls of these antechambers are decorated with everyday subjects of the kind that were already dominant in the Han period, such as a procession of officials, but are now accompanied by both Buddhist images (like the *apsaras*, celestial beings celebrating the Buddha) and Taoist themes, such as the "Seven Sages of the Bamboo Grove;" celestial images are reserved for the ceiling. The tombs were still

26

27

26. Silver gilt goblet found at Datong, Northern Wei dynasty, 4th century CE. Shaanxi, Provincial Museum.

27. Miniature temple carved from limestone for oblations, Northern Wei dynasty, about 527 CE. Boston, Museum of Fine Arts.

filled with rich grave goods, so that the soul of the deceased would not be overcome with a yearning for earthly pleasures and linger to disturb the living. From the 4th century onward, under the dynasty of the Western Jin, the lids of vases became significantly larger and helped, along with the clay statuettes, to convey the flavor of rural life and of court pastimes. From the mid-6th century onward, at the very moment when Buddhist statuary became imbued with a new solidity, funerary statuettes followed the style that had until then dominated in the Wei caves. Forms grew longer and flatter; lines were sometimes curved and animals were given implausibly thin legs in order to give them an extreme, courtly grace and slenderness.

THE MAGIC OF GLAZE

The vases found among the grave goods show a growing originality in their forms when compared with those of their "big brothers" in bronze; in the 5th century potters were better able to control their lead-based glazes. The glaze that they used was an alkaline or feldspathic (containing feldspar) coating that vitrified when heated to a high temperature.

Lead glazes had already been developed during the Han dynasty, so what were the advantages? They could be fired at low temperatures and offered a vast range of colors, depending on the impurities they contained or that were added to them deliberately. Lead glaze may have reached China through Central Asia and was known to the potters of the Mediterranean. The potters of the Sui dynasty, which was to reunite the empire, liked to give their glazes white, amber or green shades; stoneware with a green glaze (the color came from the presence of iron), known as celadon in the West, was popular in northern Zhejiang, an area that was called Yue in ancient times, and it is known by this name in China. Toward the end of the 6th century, craftsmen found a way to refine gray clay, allowing them to produce white pottery. In China, trade was carried out on a surprising scale, and the nobility were hungry for exotic refinements. Pieces of metalwork in which Central Asian and Hellenistic stylistic features can be recognized came from as far away as Persia and Bactria; archeologists have even found glass ampullae from the area of Khotan in Wei tombs. (S. B.)

29

28. Facing page: Ceramic statuette representing the bodhisattva Avalokiteśvara, Northern Qi dynasty, 563 CE. Bath, Museum of East Asian Art.

29. Glazed ceramic statuette of a camel. Tang dynasty. Toronto, Royal Ontario Museum.

30. Following pages: Terracotta statuettes of horses, Northern Wei dynasty, about 525 CE. Canada, Northern Ontario Museum.

5. China's Golden Age: the Sui and the Tang

Historians of Chinese art traditionally neglected the Sui dynasty (581-618), dismissing it as a succession of disastrous emperors. In reality its only "fault" was to precede perhaps the most flourishing dynasty in Chinese history, and one particularly astute in its propaganda: the Tang (618-907). Instead, we should look for the origins of many of the merits attributed to the Tang dynasty in the achievements of the Sui. First, they must be given all the credit for the political reunification of the empire, and for triggering the process of cultural reunion of the northern and southern populations, which had been separated for three centuries. This achievement was also a burden that — as we shall see — eventually brought down the lineage.

The dynasty lasted only two generations. The first emperor, Wendi, kept at bay the Turks who were pressing in the north. Moving from the northern plains, he conquered the southern capital Jiankang and razed it to the ground. However, he exempted his new subjects in the south from payment of taxes for ten years in order to give them time to integrate into the new political system. With the same aim in mind, he announced a new set of laws. This was the year 588. In the meantime his son and heir established an enlightened princely court at Yangzhou, acting as the patron of Buddhist and Taoist intellectuals, painters and poets: a true hothouse of culture for the decades to come. Ascending his father's throne, Yangdi used Buddhism as a means of propaganda, proclaiming himself a bodhisattva, extended Chinese influence over Southern Vietnam and attempted to subdue Korea, a dangerously expanding power. The cost of the repeated — and unsuccessful — expeditions to Korea stirred up discontent among the aristocracy. Yangdi, visionary and absolute dynast, was assassinated in a coup in 618.

CHINESE ART

143

1. Facing page: Wall of the Guan Di temple covered with Yuncheng ceramic decoration. The building was founded under the Sui dynasty and restored under the Qing.

2. Gilded bronze statuette of dragon, Tang dynasty, 7th century CE. Xi'an, Forest of Stelae Provincial Museum.

THE PURITY OF THE POTTERY

The material and visual culture of the Sui was uncovered in the 20th century, when the first tombs of the period were excavated in 1929. The grave goods included *mingqi* with a straw-yellow glaze; the palette of overglaze colors grew paler. Most of the figures immortalized in clay were musicians and dancers.

Artists of that genre were sent as a form of tribute to the Chinese emperor by the peoples of Central Asia (from Kucha, for example): they soon became vehicles of the latest courtly fashion, examples to be followed, whose hairstyles and headdresses were widely imitated. The forms and materials of the vases reveal to what extent the Sui royal house appreciated glazed stoneware, but green was no longer popular: white or buff were the preferred colors. In the north (Hebei and Henan) white pottery was produced: the aim was to create as pure a paste as possible, with or without slip, and covered with a colorless glaze; in the south (Jiangsu, Zhejiang, Sichuan, Jiangxi, Anhui) they produced green pottery (the coloring came from a paste with a lot of iron in it), covered with white slip (to mask the impurities) and a transparent glaze, creating archaic forms in imitation of bronzes.

3

3. Ceramic funerary
statuette of a horse with
green glaze, Sui dynasty,
6th-7th century CE. Berlin,
Museum für Ostasiatische
Kunst.

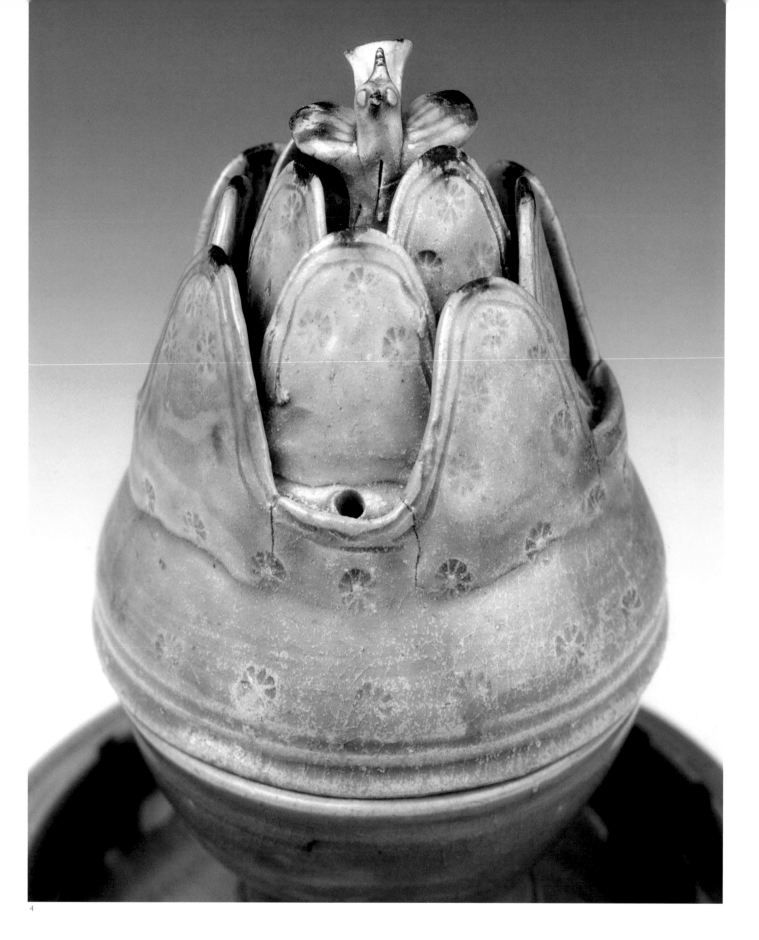

4. Ceramic incense holder
with green glaze, from
Zhejiang province, Jin
dynasty, 4th century CE.
Bath, Museum of East
Asian Art.

THE GARDEN IN THE GARDEN

Yangdi, enlightened ruler of the Sui dynasty, continued the Chinese tradition of gardening by commissioning a stunning private orchard: it contained sixteen palaces, each with its own inner garden; a *yuan zhong yuan*, a "garden in the garden," created a vista of lawns and botanical areas designed to astound and delight the observer. The Sui dynasty appears to have undertaken serial production: it was during this period that the first prints were made from wood blocks, not coincidentally canonical Buddhist texts, accompanied by sacred pictures. It was considered meritorious to produce images propagating Buddhism, and patrons soon realized that printing yielded greater merit in less time and at less expense than painting! In the same way, artists used to place huge numbers of tiny statues of the Buddha on the walls of cave temples, to convey how the Enlightened One pervaded the universe: to speed up the process, these statuettes were made from molds.

FRESCOES OF PARADISE

The walls of the Dunhuang temples of the Sui period are painted with an astonishing and fresh range of colors of mineral origin. Malachite, azurite, cinnabar and iron oxide were heavily used.

One theme appeared that would remain fundamental up until the 10th-11th century: the "Western Paradise of Amitābha." Buddhists who succeeded, through enlightenment, in escaping from the cycle of death and rebirth, could hope for a future life in a completely new cosmological order. There was a different paradise at each of the cardinal points, each one pictured as a garden in which the acolytes were admitted for eternity to the presence of their chosen Buddha, in a magnificent palace, a sort of court. Amitābha, the Buddha of Infinite Life, occupied the Western Paradise, accompanied by the bodhisattva Avalokiteśvara ("the Lord of Compassion," Guanyin in Chinese) and Mahāsthāmaprāpta (Dashizhi in Chinese). Amitābha's palace gave painters an opportunity to experiment with the representation of architecture and perspective. Landscape elements were no longer stylized. During the Sui period a happy balance was reached between the Northern Qi's fondness for plastic forms and the two-dimensionality of the pictorial illustration of the Jātaka tales of the Buddha's past lives. Painting and sculpture were integrated and fused in a visually powerful union, and the retinue surrounding the Buddha came to be represented partly in a sculptural form, partly in a painted one.

5

5. Altar of Amitābha, Sui dynasty, 584 CE, 16 in (41 cm). Xi'an, Institute for the Protection of Cultural Relics.

6. Facing page: Image of the bodhisattva Avalokiteśvara found in the Dunhuang Caves, 910 CE. London, British Museum.

7

7. Sculpture of Buddha's
disciple Ananda, Sui
dynasty, 6th century CE.
Paris, Musée National des
Arts Asiatiques-Guimet.

**8. Sculpture of the Buddha
Vairocana, Sui dynasty,
7th century CE. Paris,
Musée National des Arts
Asiatiques-Guimet.**

THE EMPIRE AT ITS PEAK: THE TANG

After Emperor Yangdi's assassination, one of his generals assumed the role of regent to his grandson. It did not take him long to seize power for himself and establish the Tang dynasty, under the name Gaozu. His son followed in his father's footsteps, eliminating his elder brothers and relegating Gaozu to a monastery. Then in 626 a ruler named Taizong ascended the throne and proved he could combine military might with civil engagement. After defeating the Turks, who were pressing on the northern frontier, he integrated many of them into the army stationed on the borders and in the capital. His generals expanded the occupied territory as far as the Tarim Basin, in what is now Kyrgyzstan; the Tang empire stretched to the Syr Darya River, in Uzbekistan. The tireless Taizong established diplomatic relations with the Tibetans who presented a threat to the west; his only failure was against the old enemy: Korea, although he conquered the island of Taiwan (then called Liuqiu), invading it with an army of 10,000 men.

The Tang poured a lot of money into the compilation of a phonetic lexicon and an encyclopedia, *Beitangshuchao*, to create a shared standard of knowledge among their subjects and help them unify after

9

9. Statue of lokapāla, guardian of tombs, Tang dynasty, 8th century CE. London, Eskenazi Collection.

10. Facing page: Statue of lokapāla, guardian of tombs, Tang dynasty, second half of the 8th century CE. Paris, Musée National des Arts Asiatiques-Guimet.

centuries of separation. Taizong created a State Office for the history of the previous dynasty, a cunning move to put historians on the sovereign's pay books – and get them to write favorably about him. When the last of the Sassanians, Yazdegerd III, had to flee Persia in 642 after a series of defeats by the Arabs, he did not set up his luxurious court in exile near Constantinople, the road to the west being barred by the Arab army. The only city in the world that allowed him to pursue the opulent lifestyle to which Baghdad had accustomed him was the capital of Taizong's empire, Chang'an, the "City of Perpetual Peace."

Chang'an, with its two million inhabitants, was certainly the New York of the 8th century: not just for the size of its population but also for its cosmopolitan nature. Its markets were packed with Persian and Sogdian warehouses; its inns were occupied by legations from all over Central Asia; its market stalls were filled with the loads of caravans from as far away as Bactria; the cavalry rode horses of unrivaled stamina and speed from distant Fergana. The city measured 42 square miles, making it a fortified center of refined civilization in the midst of the loess-covered plateau of the North China Plain.

Today all that survives of Chang'an's imposing defensive system is one section of the walls and the west gate. The median north-south axis split the city into two absolutely symmetrical halves, in which each block was assigned a function. Only two spaces escaped this rigid principle of symmetry, followed on a smaller scale by the Buddhist monasteries: the gardens and the cemeteries.

It would be left to Taizong's successor, Gaozong, to defeat Korea at last, and turn it into a foothold for spreading Chinese customs and ways in Japan too.

12

13

11. Facing page: Head of bodhisattva, Tang dynasty, 8th century CE. London, Eskenazi Collection.

12. Head of Avalokiteśvara, Tang dynasty, 7th century CE. Forest of Stelae Xi'an, Provincial Museum.

13. Statue of bodhisattva, found at Xian in 1959, Tang dynasty, 7th century CE. Xi'an, Forest of Stelae Provincial Museum.

THE SPREAD OF BUDDHISM

The Tang dynasty suffered its first jolt in 660, when Emperor Gaozong fell victim to a paralysis that resulted in almost total blindness. His concubine, Wu Zhao, seized power. Historians have not been kind in their treatment of Wu, whose gravest defect was her sex. Hoping to win her people's favor, the empress espoused the cause of Maitreya, the messianic Buddha of the future, dismissed the aristocratic elite from their public posts, and introduced the system of state examinations to pick the best brains in the country – in theory – irrespective of their rank and wealth. The imperial examinations, called *keju*, were an incred-

ible driving force for social mobility. In general, previous Tang rulers had preferred not to favor Buddhism, striving instead to create a synthesis between Buddhism, Taoism and Confucianism, although Taizong and his son, Gaozong, had established a special relationship with a famous Buddhist pilgrim, Xuanzang. However, the emperors were probably more interested in the wealth of geographical and political information gathered by the monk on his sixteen-year pilgrimage (from 629 to 645) through Central Asia and India, than in the collection of religious literature he had assembled and brought back to China. To house the 1300 volumes

I

II

I. Portrait of Princess Wu Zhao, wife of Emperor Gaozong, Tang dynasty. Paris, Musée National des Arts Asiatiques-Guimet.

II. Fresco with the Buddha Maitreya, detail, Wei dynasty, 5th century CE. Dunhuang, Mogao Caves.

of the pilgrim's library, Gaozong financed the construction of the Great Wild Goose Pagoda, a primary center for the translation of Buddhist scriptures. The pagoda has survived to this day, despite earthquakes and heavy-handed restorations.

The various fronts on which the Tang were continually engaged – in the north and Central Asia – not only resulted in the influx of various cultural influences but huge outgoings in terms of heavy military and financial commitments. Tang society was highly militarized: the military governors of the frontiers ended up taking on civil functions as well

and for forty years one male from every six families had to serve in the army.

As a product of the court milieu, the visual art that has come down to us seems preoccupied with exorcising the specter of the army through the graceful and playful splendors of palace life. But many of the generals of the army stationed on the northern borders were not Chinese, and halfway through the 8th century one of their number, a Sogdian called An Lushan, rebelled. The revolt would be put down, but only after a decade of civil war. An Lushan's rebellion marked the beginning of the

III

IV

III. Portrait of the Buddhist monk Xuanzang. London, British Museum.

IV. Great Wild Goose Pagoda, Tang dynasty, 652 CE. Xi'an.

breakdown of the Tang empire's integrity, a trauma whose long-term effects would be felt in the gloomy poetry of the 9th century, in the highly personal nature of artists' chosen themes, and in the collapse of pottery production in the north. At court the eunuchs began to exercise power, supporting first one faction and then another.

In 845, after a census of the monasteries present in the empire, the Tang ruler became aware of the immense riches in luxury goods and land that the religious bodies were keeping from the state (Buddhist structures were exempt from tax.) The emperor promptly decided to confiscate the property of the monasteries and force thousands of monks to take off their habits. The persecution affected not just the Buddhist church, but also the Nestorian and Zoroastrian ones. The empire, which had always shown a great receptiveness to foreign ideas, suddenly fell into a melancholy austerity. In one year, 845, China lost countless sacred objects made of gold and silver, confiscated by the imperial troops and melted down into ingots. Yet, as we shall see, something was spared.

In 875 the population of Henan rebelled after terrible famine. Once again a general rode the wave of unrest, using the opportunity to sweep away the eunuchs, and he found a new dynasty, the Liang. The capital was moved to Kaifeng. China turned over a new leaf.

V

V. Pagodas at the Mogao Caves.

VI. Facing page: Statue of the bodhisattva Guanyin Avalokiteśvara, Tang dynasty, 8th century CE. London, P. Goldman Collection.

SISTINE CHAPELS OF THE EAST

At the "open construction site" of Longmen, Empress Wu Zhao financed the Fengxian Temple (672-75), a three-dimensional tribute to the cult of the transcendent Buddha, Vairocana, principal deity of the Huayan sect of Buddhism. A colossal figure of Vairocana occupies the central position; at his sides are two of Buddha's closest disciples, Ananda and Kaśyapa, and two bodhisattvas; further out are two guardians of the faith, whose terrifying and martial appearance keeps at bay the enemies of Buddhism, as well as the doubts of its believers. One of these guardians, in military dress, holds a stupa, symbol of the north, for which he is responsible: so this is Vaiśravana, Bishamen or Duowen in Chinese. The cardinal points should be understood in the context of Mount Sumeru, cosmic centre of the Buddhist universe.

The sculpture is both harmonious and solid: the lips, the cheeks, even the drapery of the clothes have acquired more volume.

Dunhuang also offers us an exceptionally varied heritage of paintings. The themes most popular with patrons were the paradise of Amitābha, which had already made its appearance toward the end of the 6th century, in the Sui period, and the discussion between Mañjuśri and Vimalakīrti.

Vimalakīrti was a prosperous lay householder, profound and eloquent enough to hold his own with Buddha's best disciples in philosophical discussion and to converse with the bodhisattva Mañjuśri ("of the Beautiful Face"), the eternal sixteen-year-old patron of Buddhist gnosis (enlightenment). Naturally, patrons fond of luxury liked to identify themselves with the figure of Vimalakīrti.

From the 7th century onward the paradise of Amitābha gave artists an important opportunity to liberate themselves from the concept of walls divided into geometric rows, and, instead, to represent a story in a continuum punctuated by the landscape, by mountain ranges running diagonally across the composition, giving it height, depth and dynamism.

14

14. Statue of Buddha flanked by his disciples Ānanda and Kaśyapa and two bodhisattvas, Tang dynasty, 672-75. Longmen Caves, Fengxian Temple.

15. Statues of bodhisattva
and guardians of the faith,
Tang dynasty, 672-75.
Longmen Caves, Fengxian
Temple.

17

16. Facing page: Statue of
Vaiśravana, guardian of
the Buddhist faith, holding
a stūpa, Tang dynasty,
672-75. Longmen Caves,
Fengxian Temple.

17. Statue of Kaśyapa,
cave 419, Sui dynasty.
Dunhuang.

Study of the relationship between the characters of the Jatāka stories and the buildings in which they were set led the painters commissioned by the Buddhist monks to develop a spatial hierarchy in the composition, rather than the simple juxtaposition formerly used on the walls of tombs. The illusion of perspective in the architecture is created through a reduction in scale: the constructions grow smaller the further they are from our point of view.

The vanishing point is often high and central, so that the observer can easily contemplate the scene in all its magnificence, from a bird's eye view. The order of the central parts of the Buddhist frescoes, however, adheres to rigid iconographic conventions. There was only one way the Buddha Amitābha could be portrayed; even the geometric relationships between the polygons that make up his figure were predeter-

mined, as were the colors of the background. So it is in the peripheral areas that we must look for the artist's inspiration, for the dynamism, graphic realism, and free play of pulsating life shown in the merry-go-round of figures in the paradise of Amitābha and above all the Jatāka. Bright blue vanished from the palette of the painters at Dunhuang in the Tang period, and gradations of color were almost abandoned. Over time the forms went from rotundity to chubbiness, the decoration from crowded but balanced to chaotic and restless. The Tibetans conquered the oasis in 760; they were not driven out until 848, with the help of the Uighurs, who settled there in their turn in 873.

The Tibetans introduced a new visual influence and new iconographies, drawn from the esoteric current of Buddhism called *mi jiao*: the bodhisattva Guanyin sprouted a thousand arms and eleven heads; among

18

**18. Polychrome statues
in cave 57, Tang dynasty.
Dunhuang.**

the most popular of the other bodhisattvas was Kśitigarbha, considered capable of setting souls free from hell and giving them the chance of a rebirth. In the first few decades of Tibetan rule figures became Indianized and the composition grew more geometric.

Then with the Uighurs there was a return to an unbridled freedom, to the *horror vacui* (avoidance of empty spaces); the figures acquired Central Asian features, suggesting a rapid change in the ethnic mix of the oasis.

In 1900 Wang Yanlu, Taoist custodian of the caves at Dunhuang, largely unknown to Western scholars, discovered that one of the temples had been walled up, perhaps in the 10th century, to protect its precious contents from plunder by invaders: it proved to be a storehouse of painted and written scrolls, a cross section of the sinicized pictorial

religious art of Central Asia, perfectly preserved for our eyes, a millennium later.

The first Westerner to learn of the discovery was the British explorer Aurel Stein, who carried off the contents of the temple, some of which are now in the British Museum. Stein left a few things behind, but shortly afterward a French expedition, led by Paul Pelliot, looted the balance, which can be seen today in the Bibliothèque Nationale in Paris. The Stein collection at the British Museum includes several banners with Buddhist deities, probably used during processions: some of the figures have outlines of a fixed thickness, in a style reminiscent of the paintings "attributed" to Gu Kaizhi; others have much more dynamic outlines, with the brush tracing a thin or thick line corresponding to the grace or solidity of the figure's attitude.

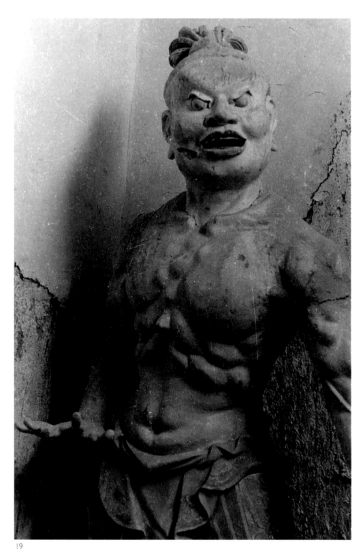

19

20

19. Devapāla warrior monk, cave 194, Tang dynasty. Dunhuang.

20. The Buddha Shakyamuni and the Buddha Prabhūtaratna conversing, cave 27, Tang dynasty. Dunhuang.

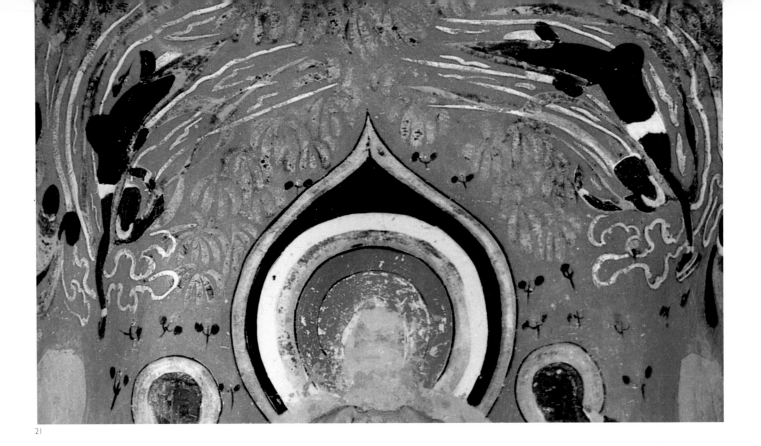

21

22

21. Fresco representing the Buddha Amitābha, detail, Tang dynasty. Dunhuang.

22. Fresco representing the paradise of Amitābha, detail of the celestial beings called *apsaras*, Tang dynasty. Dunhuang.

23. Facing page: Banner with the Buddha Shakyamuni, found by Aurel Stein in cave 17 at Dunhuang, Tang dynasty, beginning of 9th century CE. London, British Museum.

THE FASCINATION OF THE UNPREDICTABLE: THE ART OF POTTERY

In the first half of the 7th century, under the auspices of the emperor Xuanzong, a genuine technological revolution took place, resulting in incomparable elegance in two disciplines: porcelain in the proper sense of the word and *sancai* pottery.

Considerable confusion surrounds the origins of the working of porcelain, as the Chinese tend to date its invention to the 1st millennium BCE, while European scholars use a less broad definition of the term "porcelain" and claim it came into use later. Chinese porcelain has been an extraordinary catalyst for chemical research in Europe. Western rulers, captivated by the gleaming white forms of the vases produced by the Middle Kingdom, financed innumerable imitations: in Venice, for example, glass of a milky color was made.

But it was not until the 18th century that ceramicists in the electorate of Saxony realized the secret lay in the mixture of clay minerals used, one the Chinese had always found in nature, at a place called Gaoling, or "High Ridge," from which comes the term "kaolin." Kaolin is a white clay with a high fusion temperature, but has the disadvantage of being difficult to model unless combined with

25

24. Facing page: *Sancai* funerary statue of a camel, **Tang dynasty. Philadelphia, Philadelphia Museum of Art.**

25. *Sancai* vase in three colors, green, white and blue, **Tang dynasty. Bath, Museum of East Asian Art.**

other elements like silica and feldspar. Hard-paste, or real porcelain, fired at 1300°C, was first produced during the middle Tang in the 7th century CE. The earliest examples of *sancai* ceramics ("in three glazes," although more colors were actually used: green, purple, white or blue) were found in the tomb of Li Feng, who died in 674. They reached the height of their popularity in 700-50; the most fashionable forms were animals, ladies-in-waiting, horsemen, camel drivers, and wine sellers. Then *sancai* became rarer, relegated to use in burials.

How were *sancai* ceramics made? The object was subjected to a first firing at 1000-1100°C to make the biscuit; after cooling, the piece was glazed in a second firing at 900°C in an oxidizing atmosphere obtained by letting air into the kiln; finally it was covered with lead-silicate glazes colored with oxides of iron (amber-brown), copper (green), manganese and cobalt (blue).

The potter marked out areas on the surface of the vase with cuts intended to prevent the pigment from spreading out. In reality the coloring agents were not easy to control: sometimes they stayed put, sometimes they ran. But the potters relied on just this unpredictability of the glazes for their lively decoration.

27

28

26. Facing page: *Sancai* statue of a Khotanese official, Tang dynasty. Bath, Museum of East Asian Art.

27. Brown and cream vase, Tang dynasty. Private collection.

28. Upper part of a porcelain amphora with handles in the form of dragon's heads, Tang dynasty. Taipei, National Museum of History.

An Lushan's rebellion marked a watershed in the types of pottery made: the production of polychrome ceramics in the kilns of the north was drastically reduced.

Near Junzhou potters carried out the first experiments that would lead to the development of the famous Jun ware (after the name of the kiln) under the Song dynasty: stoneware with solid, stocky forms and a dark, if not black glaze. The concept underpinning the decoration was similar to that of *sancai*: the heat of the kiln was used to make the pigment run, with unpredictable and spectacular results. But the color was not obtained by strict placement of coloring agents inside frames; instead blue and white phosphatic pigments were poured over the pot.

At the city of Changsha, potters concentrated less on the quality of the mixture of clays and the elegance of the polychrome decoration; they focused their inventiveness on the original shape of the vase, influenced by examples of metal vessels from Central Asia.

29

29. Ceramic vessel in the form of a mythological animal, from Changsha, Tang dynasty, late 9th century CE. Bath, Museum of East Asian Art.

30. Facing page: *Celadon* vase decorated with a pattern of lotus flowers, Tang dynasty, 10th century CE. Bath, Museum of East Asian Art.

MINUTE MASTERPIECES, COLOSSAL CUSTODIANS

As usual, we must start from the world of the dead to understand the art of the living. The Tang royal house no longer built artificial hills for its tombs but made use of those present in nature, which represented a considerable saving. Archeologists have identified an area of imperial tombs near a tributary of the Wei River. The burial chambers remain inviolate, but the *shen dao*, the sacred avenues leading to the mausoleums of Taizong and of Gaozong are clearly visible. Not far from the impressive statues that line these access routes lies the corridor in the hill leading to the tomb of Princess Yongtai, one of seventeen laid out around Gaozong's last resting place. Troublesome daughter of a future emperor, Yongtai was quickly disposed of, murdered at the age of seventeen. Whoever prepared her grave goods understood the nature of the calculating court at which she spent her brief existence. The walls of the tomb illustrate events at court with precise delicacy, the

figures are arranged in orderly fashion, conveying the various movements of the throng and depicting the idiosyncratic expressions of each face. The black limestone sarcophagus is engraved with scenes of the princess's daily life, in which the artist has also tried his hand at portraying some figures almost from the back. The space occupied by Yongtai's servants, surrounding their mistress, is flattened, with little depth, as if to increase the sense of intimacy between maids of honor and princess. The *mingqi* even represent a polo match, a popular pastime at court in which both men and women took part: Yongtai may have been among them, as one of the statuettes appears to show her striking the ball, displaying the total concentration typical of adolescents engaged in competition. What is certain is that the princess was buried in an iconic, eternal version of her intimate diary. Its discrete elegance is in stark contrast to the immobile, labored rhetoric of the imperial tombs.

The Tang *mingqi*, made in molds from red, gray or buff clay and up

31

31. Statue of winged bull near the tomb of Princess Wu Zhao at Qianling, Tang dynasty, 8th century CE. Shaanxi.

32. Facing page: Antechamber of the tomb of Princess Yongtai at Qianling, Tang dynasty, first half of 8th century CE. Shaanxi.

to three feet or one meter high, retain a touching vivacity, reflecting the sculptors' great feeling for the tense posture, the "freeze frame" of the gesture, the spring, the leap, the smile: horses start in irritation, camels weep with exhaustion, Persian traders deal in wine, taking sips from the jar. As the decades pass the damsels grow increasingly plump, adapting to new canons of female beauty; and, of course, the young men play polo, the last celebration of life before the tomb is closed to the gaze of the living. The mythical animals defending the tomb remain terrifying. If the client were sufficiently wealthy, then the ceramicist added glaze, protecting the figures and giving them an attractive luster. They would then be painted minutely, over the glaze and without firing, thereby enabling the process to be better controlled, in lively colors and with a fine brush. If the patron were very wealthy, some ornaments of the dress might even be gilded.

Why were the *mingqi* colored over glaze? An underglaze coloring would have run when fired, producing effects that looked fine on pots, but were undesirable for figures; it was not until the Liao dynasty that potters learned to control underglaze coloring better. Unfortunately the overglaze coloring of the clay statuettes has almost totally vanished today.

After the Tang dynasty, *mingqi* went into gradual decline, eventually going out of fashion entirely, partly as a result of the spread of cremation under the Ming dynasty, when paper objects that could be burned with the corpse were used.

33

33. Black limestone sarcophagus of Princess Yongtai, Tang dynasty, first half of 8th century CE. Xi'an, Forest of Stelae Provincial Museum.

34. Facing page: Glazed ceramic statuettes found in the tomb of Princess Yongtai at Qianling, Tang dynasty, first half of 8th century CE. Shaanxi.

35

35. Ceramic funerary statuette of a polo player, Tang dynasty. London, Sotheby's Auction House.

36. Facing page: *Sancai* funerary statuette of an official, Tang dynasty. London, Christie's Auction House.

WOODEN SKYSCRAPERS: RELIGIOUS ARCHITECTURE

The daring religious architecture of the Tang has been preserved in the temples built in imitation in Japan – the Shitennō-ji, Horyu-ji and Yakushi-ji – but very little has survived in its homeland. The oldest wooden construction to have been preserved is the Foguangsi on Mount Wutai.

In general the layout of a Buddhist monastery consisted of an area bounded by walls, through which visitors followed a route usually oriented from south to north. Entering through a gateway to the south, they proceeded toward the pagoda, storehouse of the temple relics, behind which was located the golden hall where the Buddhist triad was worshipped.

In the Foguangsi we can distinguish a bipartite division, between terracing and pagoda: the terrace performed a symbolic function, recalling

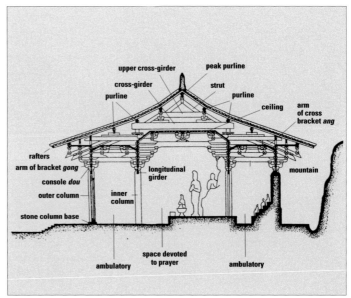

38

39

37. Facing page: Hōryū-ji Temple. Ikaruga, Nara prefecture, Japan.

38. Section of the main pavilion of the *Foguangsi*, Tang dynasty. Mount Wutai.

39. Hōryū-ji Temple, view of the golden hall. Ikaruga, Nara prefecture, Japan.

Mount Sumeru, the center of Indian cosmogony, as well as meeting the practical need to house the crowd of devotees during public services. To understand the function and origin of the pagoda, however, we should remember that on the death of the Buddha, in the 6th century BCE, his body was cremated on a funeral pyre; the few remaining bones were shared out among his disciples, who scattered them over the Indian soil. When the disciples reached a region where people were receptive to their preaching, they buried the relic of the Buddha in their possession and built a cenotaph (an "empty tomb") over it, the stupa. The monastic community grew up around it, and above it rose a reliquary tower, commonly called a pagoda, derived via Portuguese from the Singhalese word *dagoba*, meaning a shrine holding Buddhist relics. The form of the pagoda is the result of the synthesis of the *śikara* (the superstructure of an Indian temple) and the *lou* (the Chinese military watchtower), in place from the 3rd century CE on.

The roof of the *Foguangsi* pagoda still offers a splendid example of the *dou gong* system of beams and purlins, whose slope increases in relation to the height of the supported roof: this makes it possible for the roof to project a long way out, with the last section rising and turning outward. Each dynasty improved and complicated this system of brackets, so that a building can be approximately dated from an examination of its *dou gong*. At Xian, the former Chang'an, capital of the empire, we find one of the oldest examples of a pagoda built of masonry, *Dayanda*, the Great Wild Goose Pagoda (there is also a Little Wild Goose Pagoda, a bit more out of the way but still in the capital: with its curved silhouette, it surpasses the other in grace and dynamism, but not in age). The embedded pillars that punctuate each floor reveal how the architect was inspired by earlier wooden equivalents: they have no supporting function but imitate their predecessors, and animate the surface of the pagoda with the repeated design.

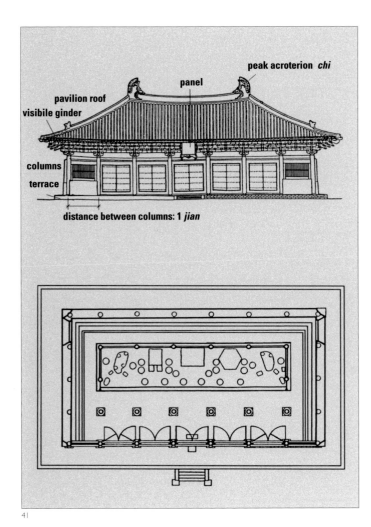

41

42

40. Facing page: Great Wild Goose Pagoda built around 652 CE and restored under the Qing dynasty. Xi'an.

41. Elevation and plan of the main pavilion of the *Foguangsi*, Tang dynasty.

42. Little Wild Goose Pagoda. Xi'an.

THE GREAT TANG PAINTERS

We can follow the taste of the great Tang collectors thanks to the works of contemporary art historians: in 847 Zhang Yanyuan wrote *Lidai minghua ji* ("Famous Paintings through History"), in the same century Zhu Jingxuan wrote *Tangchao minghua lu* ("Famous Paintings of the Tang Dynasty") and as early as the mid-7th century Pei Xiaoran, complying with the Tang passion for compilation and cataloging, composed the *Zhenguan gongsihua lu* ("Catalog of the Paintings of Imperial and Private Collections in the Zhenguan Era", i.e. 627-49, practically the years of Taizong's reign).

But – apart from religious art, at Dunhuang – not even a single painting by this kaleidoscope of painters has been preserved.

We know that around 750 Su Zong founded the Hanlin Yuan, the "Brush Wood Court," an academy established to fund the studies of a number of scholars (including painters) who acted as advisers to the emperor. By this time Chang'an was already a cosmopolitan city, in which for example a family from Khotan, the Yuzhi, was able to run a workshop for several generations. They were celebrated portraitists, who made little use of the typically Chinese outline and were extremely popular with their clients because of the vivid way they portrayed the subject through the use of repeated applications of paint, giving the picture an almost three-dimensional character. We know the name of Wu Daozi, a great religious artist, celebrated for the vigor of his brushwork: his figures were said to have the breath of life, but even in the 11th century very few of his original paintings were in circulation. The palace kept

43

43. *Man Herding Horses*
in the style of Han Gan,
Tang dynasty, 8th century
CE. Taipei, National
Palace Museum.

44

huashi, court painters, at its disposal, paying them to immortalize the curious faces of ambassadors and their gifts, often animals, or the patriarchs of the various religious sects. One very famous painting depicts Night-Shining White, one of the prize horses in the stables of Emperor Xuanzong; the horse seems to shy – while still tethered – before our eyes, evidently disturbed by the presence of the painter scrutinizing it. Much of the picture is a restoration carried out in the 12th century, but the head and withers may be the work of Han Gan, a sort of Chinese Giotto, who worked in a wine shop. The great painter Wang Wei (of whose work no trace remains) and his brother frequented the shop and used to buy wine on credit before a heavy night's drinking; Han Gan then had to go to Wang Wei's house to ask for payment. Wang Wei saw him drawing figures and horses in the sand while he was waiting; and the artist, impressed by the boy's talent, took him on as a pupil.

Summoned to court, Han Gan displayed a style all of his own, telling the intrigued emperor: "I have my private teachers: the horses in your majesty's collection." In reality, for Han Gan painting horses was an opportunity to paint their owners as well: we know that he was also a renowned portraitist. But for us his name remains linked to horses, even though these subjects were always handled in a fairly two-dimensional,

flat way. Perhaps only one painter whose name we know has escaped the cruel ravages of time: Li Zhen. Curiously neglected in his own country, he painted portraits of Buddhist patriarchs. Pilgrims often bought his works, as did Kōbō Daishi, founder of the Shingon sect in Japan, before returning home from China in 804. He took with him portraits by Li Zhen of the five patriarchs of his sect and deposited them at the Tō Temple in Kyoto. Miraculously, those portraits have survived. Measuring 33.1 × 23.6 in (84 × 60 cm), each portrait comprises an image, the title and the biography of the patriarch. All the figures are lightly represented in half profile, their plasticity, their mass, clearly articulated.

In the landscapes painted on the walls of Dunhuang we discover a variety of methods: a more linear approach, where the artist lays on areas of fairly dilute paint and then goes over the outlines of the objects with a thick and even brushstroke, creating the impression of "filled boundaries;" a "boneless" depiction, where the colors are less bright and the outline thinner; and finally a more authentically pictorial approach, where there is no outline at all but the forms are represented by color alone. From later copies of the masterpieces of Wang Wei, it seems that the painter preferred this last technique. Taizong set great store by calligraphy: one-third of the way through the 7th century he

44. Han Gan, *The Horse Night-Shining White*, 8th century CE (much of the painting is a restoration carried out in the 12th century CE), 12.1x13.4 in (30.8x34 cm). New York, Metropolitan Museum of Art.

set up two academies of calligraphy, one for the imperial house and the other for high officials. He assembled a collection of the best works in the empire; where the imperial seizures could not reach, he had copies made, by means of a kind of "lithographic" reproduction of the image. Stone matrices were prepared for the masterpieces, on which highly skilled stonecutters used their scalpels to imitate the soft movements of the brush in the original. A film of charcoal was spread over the stone, a sheet of paper was applied and pressed with a pad: a copy of

45

46

45-46. *The Hundred Horses*, scroll in the style of Han Gan, whole and detail, Tang dynasty, 10.5x118.9 in (26.7x302.1 cm). Beijing, Palace Museum.

the original calligraphy was left on the paper, in white on black. A stone rubbing of this kind has preserved a work by Yan Zhenqing, the *Yan Family Temple Stele*, in which the artist uses a regular script in vigorous brushstrokes of great thickness. Zhang Xu (who lived between 713 and 740) conducted new experiments with cursive script, creating the *kuang caoshu*, a mixture of regular and cursive. His disciple was the

47

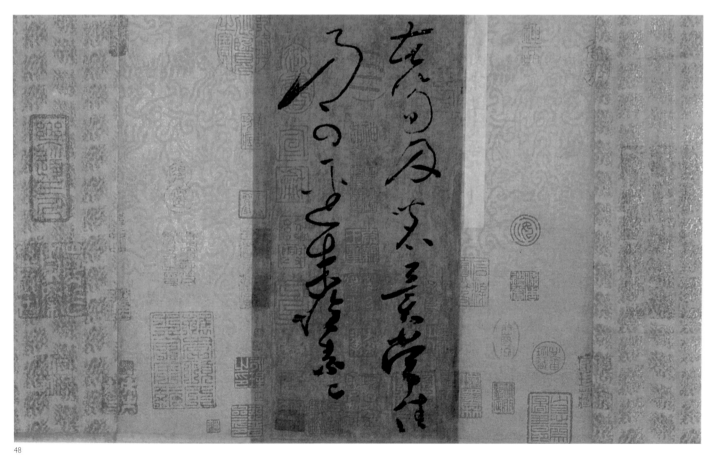

48

47. Zhou Fang, section of a scroll representing ladies and servants, copy from the Song period, 13.3x80.6 in (33.7x204.8 cm). Beijing, Palace Museum.

48. Huaisu, section of a scroll in wild cursive, Tang dynasty, second half of 8th century CE. Shanghai, Shanghai Museum.

brilliant Huaisu, whose secular name was Qian Cangzhen; he became a Buddhist monk, traveled the length and breadth of the empire and humbly followed the advice of older calligraphers. Four of his works have survived, but his masterpiece is his *Autobiography*, in which the account of his own life, his Buddhist vocation and his aesthetic choices are fused in a cursive script of overwhelming beauty.

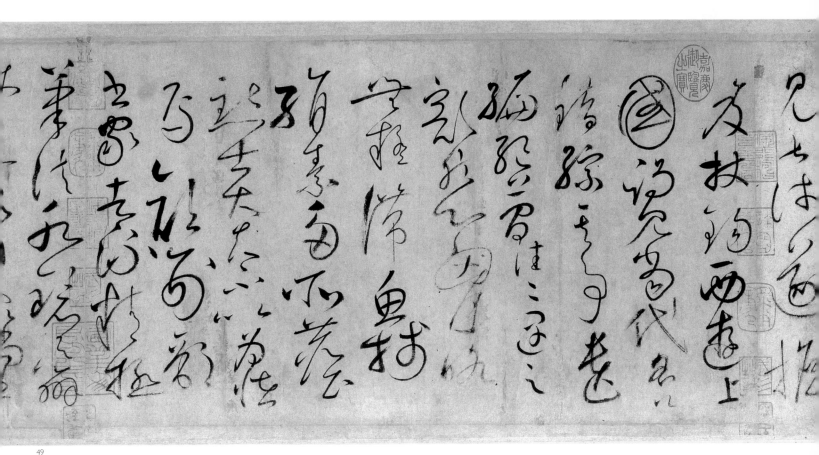

49. Huaisu, part of *Autobiography*, Tang dynasty, 725-85 CE, 11.1x297.2 in (28.3x755 cm). Taipei, National Palace Museum.

Zhou Fang (780-810) specialized in women of opulent beauty – the kind preferred by Tang aesthetics. In the copies of his paintings that have come down to us (from the Song period) the woman is no longer depicted dancing or dining, but generally alone, absorbed in her housework. When we see groups of damsels in movement, they do so with discretion, not heat and passion. Zhao Zong, a high-ranking member of the government, commissioned a portrait from Han Gan and Zhou Fang. When he showed the results to his wife, she commented: "They are both good likenesses; but Zhou Fang's captures your character, your smile, your words." So Zhao Zong lavished scrolls of silk on Zhou Fang – at the time silk, given its value and uniqueness, was used as a form of payment, almost preferred to bars of silver. Zhou Fang creates a sense of space not by an arrangement of furniture, as in the rare examples of earlier paintings, but through the relationship of the figures with one another. What is fascinating about the women depicted by Zhou is their concentration. They are "absorbed," and this is the key to the artist's work: his figures are always engrossed in something within the composition, perhaps playing music or weaving, and it is a vortex into which we too are drawn. The distribution of the figures in space becomes silence, helping to heighten the concentration. If the dimensions of the furniture surprise us, we have to remember that chairs were not used in the Tang period: people sat on carpets, so tables and dressers were low.

I. Facing page: *The Palace Ladies Washing Children*, detail, copy after Zhou Fang, early 12th century CE. New York, Metropolitan Museum of Art.

II. *Tuning the Lute and Drinking Tea*, detail, copy after Zhou Fang, 12th century CE, 11x29.6 in (28x75.3 cm). Kansas City, Nelson Atkins Museum of Art.

III. Zhou Fang, *Ladies Playing Double Sixes*, 8th century CE.

Some of the finest examples of Tang bronze work are mirrors. The front of the mirror was polished to reflect the image of its user; an eyelet – sometimes in the form of a crouching animal – was set on the back to hold a ribbon; the surrounding space was filled with a flamboyant decoration: palmettes, birds, butterflies and dragonflies, or bunches of grapes. The vine motif, popular in the Han period (when it was brought to China for the first time by the explorer Zhang Qian), came back into vogue under the Sui dynasty, as it echoed the patterns used on Sassanid textiles. In some cases the decoration on the back was embellished with silver damascening.

As well as being an essential part of every lady's toilet, the mirror was worn on the belt, as a protection against malicious influences, or hung in the bedchamber as a symbol of marital fidelity.

In October 1970 two jars filled with treasure were found at Hejiacun,

51

50. Bronze mirror with decoration in relief representing a tiger carrying seven cubs, Tang dynasty. Berlin, Museum für Ostasiatische Kunst.

51. Silver earrings in the form of a dragon, Tang dynasty. London, Eskenazi Gallery.

on the outskirts of Xian: they held coins, not just from China but from Japan, Persia, Central Asia and Rome, as well as almost three hundred gold and silver objects, dozens of silver ingots, three pieces of agate ware and a *sancai* vase; there were also rare medicinal herbs, reserved for the emperor's use, pharmaceutical instruments and a container for perfumes in gold and silver. Where did it all come from? In 783, fearing a coup in the capital, a high-ranking official called Liu Zhen, in charge of the imperial vault, buried the treasure and fled the city.

Clearly he succeeded in saving the objects but not his life, as he never returned to reclaim the jars, which now offer us a glimpse of the cosmopolitan luxury enjoyed at court. The influence of Sassanid Persian metalwork can be seen in the details, such as the punching used to decorate the silver cups.

In the 1980s, a landslip undermined the foundations of the pagoda of the Famensi Temple, about 12 miles (20 kilometers) from Xian. During the restoration work, archeologists realized that the foundations

52

53

52. Sacred gold work, from the Famensi Pagoda, Tang dynasty. Shaanxi, Famensi Museum, Fufeng.

53. Gold casket for jewels, from the Famensi Pagoda, Tang dynasty. Shaanxi, Famensi Museum, Fufeng.

concealed a cell, a sort of strong room in which the monks had placed their sacred vestments and ornaments to protect them from plunder by local brigands in 874. Among the objects brought to light in April 1987 was a finger bone reputed to be that of the Buddha, which the monks used to carry in procession once a year to the capital, where they received gifts from the court. The cell also contained the votive offerings of the Tang rulers, including rock crystal, glass, 7000 bolts of silk and fourteen vases of a type known from the texts but of which

no trace had previously been found: *miseci*, or "secret-color" Yue ware, decorated with slip in a pale shade of green and as smooth as silk. Previously, the most common type of Yue glaze had been a yellowish-green celadon. The pottery from the Famensi has a completely different tone. "Secret-color" Yue ware makes us even more painfully aware of the fact that a vase "dies" when placed in the showcase of a museum, losing one of its fundamental qualities, the pleasure it gives to the sense of touch. *(S. B.)*

54

55

54. Sacred gold work, from the Famensi Pagoda, Tang dynasty. Shaanxi, Famensi Museum, Fufeng.

55. "Secret-color" Yue vase, from the Famensi Pagoda, Tang dynasty. Shaanxi, Famensi Museum, Fufeng.

6. The Five Dynasties and the Liao

After the fall of the Tang the conflict between various contenders for the imperial throne lasted more than half a century, from 907 to 960. Over this time five different royal houses succeeded one another in the capital Nanjing; in the northern province, outside the control of the main court, a new kingdom was established every ten years. For this reason the period is traditionally known to Chinese historians as that of the "Five Dynasties and Ten Kingdoms."

Apart from these dynastic upheavals, the Han, the Chinese people proper, lost their grip on the far north, where new nomadic powers appeared: the Khitan and the Western Xia. The Khitan came from the valley of the Liao River, from which their dynasty (907-1125) took its name. The Xia extended their rule over a very large territory, from the Ordos River to what is now Gansu province, and prospered from their control of the caravan routes, trading chiefly in cattle, wax, and carpets. The Song dynasty, which reestablished the unity of the empire, was obliged to buy peace by paying tribute, the only way it could stave off military pressure on the northern frontier. The annual missions sent by the nomads to the Chinese court to collect payment (in precious metal as well as goods like silk) provided a special opportunity for encounters and exchange of visual influences between the cultures of the two peoples. As often happened, the nomads were fascinated by the opulence and solidity of Chinese tradition and, with their customary vivacity, absorbed it rapidly.

1. Facing page: Painting on silk of Vaiśravana, Guardian of the North, detail, from cave 17 at Dunhuang, Five Dynasties period, mid-10th century. London, British Museum.

2. Crown, Liao dynasty, 907-1125 CE. Hohhot, Inner Mongolia Museum.

THE COURTS OF CHENGDU AND NANJING

The political fragmentation of this period accelerated the development of regional artistic traditions. The protagonists of this decentralization were the court at Chengdu, capital of the kingdom of Shu (corresponding to the modern province of Sichuan), and the court at Nanjing, capital of the Later Tang dynasty (which ruled until 975 and was then absorbed by the Song), whose last emperor, Li Houzhu, was a highly sensitive patron. The Song inherited an extremely sophisticated enclave of culture from him.

The northern kingdoms, which gravitated around the city of Kaifeng, were weaker courts with a less lively culture, although it was precisely this area that gave birth to a school of landscape painting that was to have a long and impressive tradition.

The 10th and 11th centuries saw a gradual but permanent shift in power: leadership passed from the military and landed aristocracy to an elite of officials and scholars. The visual approach, in the most diverse arts, shifted from the static and decorative to the dynamic.

3

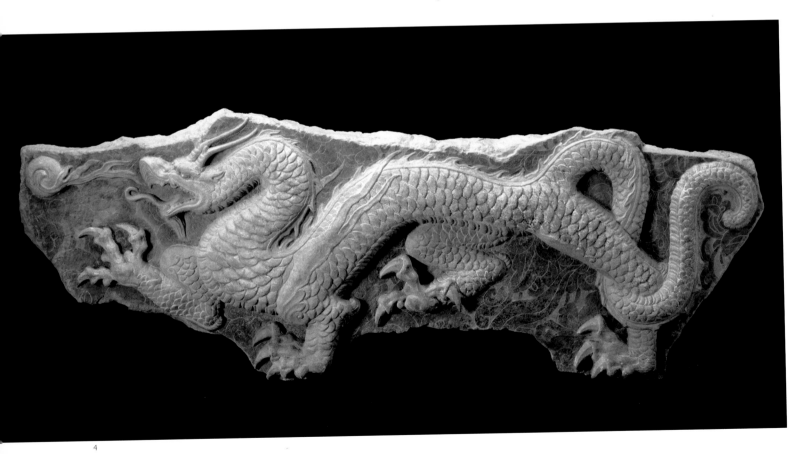

4

3. Yao bowl with five petals in *celadon* **pottery, Five Dynasties period, 10th century. Bath, Museum of East Asian Art.**

4. Relief with dragon, Five Dynasties period, 907-60 CE. Indianapolis, Museum of Art.

5. Facing page: Cosmetics holder in celadon pottery, Five Dynasties period or Northern Song dynasty, 10th-11th century CE. Bath, Museum of East Asian Art.

become popular again in the 17th century, thanks to the genius of a few painters who broke away from the Qing tendencies, earning themselves the title of "individualists."

Commercial Buddhist painting, the diametrical opposite of Chan sobriety, flourished. Centered at the port of Ningbo, in Zhejiang, it was an almost industrial art, churning out uninspired and brightly colored images for the faithful. In this period the technique of printing from woodblocks in three colors (blue, red and yellow) was also developed, specifically to keep up with the demand for sacred Buddhist images from pilgrims and increase their appeal.

It is not always easy to assign the individual painters of the period to one dynasty or another: it was common for a painter to start his career at one court and then, after its conquest by a rival royal house, be invited to move to another capital. Many of these artists lived through several of these continual upheavals. Such displacements of cultural milieus encouraged curiosity and comparison: the different regional schools, which for decades had been the breeding grounds of independent traditions, now had the opportunity to fuse, accelerating the emergence of new formal approaches. Take, for instance, the school of Nanjing. Around 975, the Song ruler threatened the city with his army. Given that the end was imminent, all the emperor of the Later Tang, Li Houzhu, could do was swallow the bitter pill, and so he decided to send the following message to the besieger: "I regard you as a father." The reply of the future Song emperor, Taizu, was pitiless: "But children do not escape from their parents. And do you think I would let another man snore in my bed at my side?"

An inglorious end for Li, the scrupulous patron who brought the Hanlin Yuan, the Brush Wood Academy, back to life. He was even meticulous in the choice of the paper he wrote on, which he had made for the purpose.

9

9. Gu Hongzhong, *Five Flute Players*, fourth scene from the *Night Banquet of Han Xizai*, Five Dynasties period, 907-60 CE. Beijing, Palace Museum.

Seeing that the end was nigh Han Xizai, chief minister of his government, had spent everything he had left on buying a hundred or so slaves and throwing orgiastic parties. In an attempt to rehabilitate him, the emperor sent a painter from the academy as a spy, with instructions to immortalize the debauched participants. The emperor's hope was that, with a mirror held up to his vice, his minister would repent. But Han no longer had any faith in the future, and did not bat an eyelid.

The Night *Banquet of Han* Xizai scroll – a sort of reportage ahead of its time – did not serve its purpose, but it does convey to us intact, with the urgency of a masterpiece, the refinement of 10th-century Nanjing in all its freshness. There is some question as to whether the painting is not in fact a Song copy. But the painter is traditionally identified as Gu Hongzhong, originally from Jiangnan. He came up with a dramatic scenario: divans, beds and screens separate the episodes, in which the master of the house appears several times; in the first illustration we see

10

11

10. Gu Hongzhong, *The Dance of Wang Wushan*, second scene from the *Night Banquet of Han Xizai*, Five Dynasties period, 907-60 CE. Beijing, Palace Museum.

11. Gu Hongzhong, scene from the *Night Banquet of Han Xizai*, Five Dynasties period, 907-60 CE. Beijing, Palace Museum.

a detail of the fourth scene, dominated by five flautists accompanied by a castanet player. The artist concentrates the bitterness he feels over the decadence of the period into the last scene, where a young man tries to persuade a girl to join the orgy. This snapshot of his time, in a last flicker of discretion, does not tell us whether the girl yields. Shortly afterward, the dynasty was to fall.

Another great artist of the age, Xu Xi, was also active at the court in Nanjing. We know that he painted almost exclusively bamboo (the only plant, apart from the plum and the pine, that ever interested scholarly painters). The painting *Snow Covers Bamboo* is usually attributed to him, but in reality its author is unknown. Xu used hard brushes and subdued colors.

In this scroll the artist uses a sparing technique: the highlights on the plants are obtained by leaving the paper blank. Thus the brushstrokes do not have to contribute to the construction of the part of the bamboo "in positive": they depict not the material, but its shadow. So the artist's approach to representation is the complete opposite of the usual one. Xu Xi's painstaking accuracy and constancy met with immediate success: his works entered the imperial collections while he was still alive.

Indeed, hidden on one of the stems is an inscription (upside down) declaring "*this bamboo is worth more than a thousand pieces of gold.*" We must hope that it was not written by the artist himself, but was the discreet comment of some contemporary collector.

Unfortunately the gloomy genius of Xu Xi, which made him stand out from his contemporaries, resulted in the abrupt disappearance of his style, as he took no disciples. By an irony of fate, his progeny devoted themselves to academic painting, whose technical premises were completely different.

What was the dominant style in academic painting? In its first century, the Song Academy had taken as its point of reference the work of Huang Quan, an artist active at the court of Chengdu, in the kingdom of Shu, some time between 900 and 965. An enthusiastic observer of fauna, especially birds, he traced the outline of his subject with a vigorous brushstroke, but instead of using lines to represent the articulation of the limbs, he relied on a series of thin veils of color.

It is said that some ambassadors to Chengdu brought an eagle as a gift to the king, and that the bird of prey had swooped on the neck of a pheasant. Unfortunately for its beak, the pheasant was not running

13

12. Facing page: Xu Xi, (attrib.), *Snow Covers Bamboo,* **mid-10th century CE, 59.4x39 in (151x99 cm). Shanghai, Shanghai Museum.**

13. Huang Quan, *Sketches of Rare Animals Portrayed from Life,* **Southern Song dynasty, 10th century CE, 16.1x27.6 in (41x70 cm). Beijing, Palace Museum.**

CHINESE ART

around the court, but painted on the wall of the palace by the inimitable hand of Huang Quan. Anecdotes of this kind are common in Chinese biographies of artists, and are used to suggest an illusionism so effective that it could deceive nature herself.

In *Sketches of Rare Animals Portrayed from Life* the artist expresses the wonder of a child at the variety of forms taken by life. He is attracted by reptiles (the tortoise) and by everything that is extremely small but complex (insects); he joyfully investigates the myriad poses and tints of birds. Although the figures are juxtaposed as if they were a collection of samples, each one stands out solidly, set in space with no uncertainty of the painter's hand. Indeed, each animal suggests and redefines the space around it with its posture.

These two album-pages probably constitute a sort of miscellany of the painter's direct observations: we can imagine him peering intently to capture the details of his subjects, or pondering which pigment to use for an elytron (an insect's forewing) or a wing. The pages were then remounted as a scroll, bearing the inscription, "for the studies of my son Ju Bao." And it was his son who brought his style to the Song Academy in Kaifeng, where it soon came to be known as *fugui* ("rich and aristo-cratic") in contrast to the *yeyi* ("free and wild") style of Xu Xi.

It was inevitable that Xu's monochrome work and Huang's naturalistic style would be viewed by posterity as hard to reconcile. The passion that Huang put into teaching made him better-known over the medium term, given that – as we have seen – Xu did not invest any energy in the training of followers.

Jing Hao painted in the first half of the 10th century. He was born in the north, at Jinshui in Henan, but spent much of his life as a farmer in the Taihang Mountains.

The paintings that were unhesitatingly attributed to Jing Hao in the past are in reality the work of a whole range of artists, something which has left us with a somewhat distorted impression of his style. The one common characteristic, looking at *Mount Lu* for example, is the monu-mentality of his compositions. He used a rather monotonous range of brushstrokes, meticulous but not very varied. Although the overall composition appears rather confused, due to the multiplicity of details, the eye is drawn strongly toward the horizon by diagonal lines of force, running from bottom left to top right, of ever greater depth. The sense of distance is conveyed through the superimposition of forms; color is absent. The uneven path is a twofold expedient: it links separate areas of the composition together and suggests a before and an after, an "out-side" not included in the frame, increasing the breadth of the picture.

Jing had a peculiar quirk: he signed his paintings at obscure points, such

14

14. Jing Hao,
Mount Lu, **9th-10th**
century CE, 73.6x42.1
in (187x107 cm). Taipei,
National Palace Museum.

as on the surface of a boulder. He wrote a treatise in the form of a dialogue, *Hua Shanshui Lu* (*Painting Landscapes*); in it he imagines that an old hermit on Mount Taishan (where he had lived as a farmer) is interrogated by an aspiring young landscape painter. We would expect the former to personify Jing Hao: curiously, he identifies more with the latter.

Li Cheng (919-67) was born at Chang'an, but took refuge with his family in Shandong when the Song took the city by storm in 957. He spent his days indulging in his three great passions: wine, music and chess. Judging by this, it might seem that he was not destined to achieve much, but the sources tell us that he passed the *jinshi* exams, and so must have devoted a lot of time (between playing games and music and drinking) to study of the Confucian classics. In reality, during his life he did not decline contact with Chan Buddhist circles, where he learned the practice of meditation.

A kinsman who became governor of Kaifeng bought up his paintings at very high prices, hoarding his output and greatly reducing the number of scrolls in circulation. It soon became difficult to track down an authentic Li Cheng. The Song empress Cisheng Guangxian (the wife of Renzong) managed to get hold of all the Li Cheng paintings still available, and remounted them to form a screen. Not even this, which must have comprised a series of masterpieces, has survived.

Like Dong Yuan's *Xiao and Xiang Rivers*, Li Cheng's A Solitary *Temple amid Clearing Peaks* starts out from water, but goes on to convey quite another sensation, an absolute verticality; the higher the eye goes in the composition, the more everything seems to be drawn upward. In the foreground men are bent under the weight of their daily labors; then a monastery is set on a knoll, portrayed with dry, meticulous brushwork; the temple stands at the precise center of the scroll. But a simple mountain towers over this display of man's constructive ingenuity, the eight-story pagoda, cutting it down to size. Further back, in even lighter ink so as to suggest a greater distance, a still higher peak diminishes the summit that had seemed so overwhelming. As the altitude increases, even the trees change from threatening shrubs, becoming vertical ticks, in union with unspoiled nature. The brushstroke – the Chinese master's weapon – also grows more and more tapered. A good half of the composition, some 2 feet or 60 centimeters of silk, is devoted to this second part, to nature empty of human presence.

Fan Kuan was from the northern territories; he was born at Hu Yuan in Shaanxi and lived from around 950 to 1020. Kuan was not his real name: it was a *nom de plume* meaning "the Vast," referring to the breadth of his landscapes. At some point in his development he stopped using

15

15. Li Cheng, *A Solitary Temple amid Clearing Peaks*, 10th century CE, 44.1x22 in (112x56 cm). Kansas City, Nelson-Atkins Museum of Fine Arts.

THE LIAO

Khitan artists introduced a whole series of innovations into the themes of Chinese art. These nomads were not at all interested in idealizing their subject, but instead sought to capture their individuality, the uniqueness of their personalities. Fervent Buddhists (the Khitan had five capitals, one for each cardinal point of the Tantric cosmogony), they left us masterpieces in the fields of religious architecture and statuary, in bronze, ceramic and wood.

18

19

18. Gilded bronze statue of a bodhisattva seated on a lotus blossom, Liao dynasty, mid-11th century CE. Bath, Museum of East Asian Art.

19. Statue of bodhisattva in lacquered wood, Liao dynasty, 9th-10th century CE. Toronto, Royal Ontario Museum.

The popularity of Khitan paintings at the Chinese court was due to their exoticism and to the vivid way in which they portrayed some subjects, now grown less familiar in the Middle Kingdom, such as the stag. This last was the pivot of the work of Li Zanhua (899-936), eldest son of the founder of the Liao dynasty, Abaoji. Judging by the typically Chinese surname with which he is recorded in the chronicles, Li, it appears that the Song court had been happy to indulge the young man's inclination for painting in order to snare him in its own sphere of influence through the powerful Chinese tradition of visual art.

Hu Gui spoke Chinese, brooded on Chinese culture … but in reality was a Khitan, and thus a nomad who had adopted a sedentary life. He painted chiefly camels and horses, using brushes of wolf hair to give his subjects more life; yet the texture he used renders the brushwork almost invisible, imparting a particular softness to the coats of the animals and the landscape in which they are set. He often chose to depict open spaces dotted with horsemen in complicated poses. This predisposition for original genre scenes found a parallel in the tombs of the Liao, where we find murals of striking vivacity. In a *trompe-l'oeil*, a maidservant is half-concealed by the door of a closet she is opening; the artist takes advantage of this to linger over the decoration of the closet, lacquered in red and decorated with golden phoenixes. In the same tomb there is a scene of the preparation of a banquet, set inside a framework of mock beams that is also used to divide up the various murals. Two men are serving themselves drinks; the pieces of crockery are depicted with such precision that we can recognize a type in vogue at the time, a sort of carafe united with a saucer. Represented on a smaller scale, since they are less important,

20

21

20. *Woman Opening a Door,* fresco from the tomb of Zhang Shiqing, Liao dynasty. Xuanhua, Hebei province.

21. *Preparation of a Banquet,* fresco from the tomb of Zhang Shiqing, Liao dynasty. Xuanhua, Hebei province.

two maids are bustling in the doorway, at the side. These murals are invaluable aids to reconstructing the fashions and hairstyles of the period, always represented in great detail.

The theme of fondness for the warmth of the hearth fills the walls of the Liao tombs, as if the desire were to surround the deceased with everyday activities that took place in the bosom of the family: one painter has amused himself by depicting children at play, laughing behind the backs of servants trying to cope with the whims of their mistress. We see a table for study, a stand for pottery, a family pet dashing into the scene, attracted by the commotion or by a butterfly fluttering unconcerned into the midst of the squabble between servants. One of the boys rests his hand on the head of his friend, in a lively gesture of spontaneous camaraderie – or perhaps to stop him from revealing himself too soon to the butts of their joke.

A wooden wall offers us an extremely delicate example of *niao hua* ("flowers and birds") painting, which we would be tempted to call a still life if it were not for the fact that the Chinese have always preferred to depict nature on the move, in all its tension. In *Mating Cries*

22

22. *Children Playing*,
fresco from the tomb
of Zhang Wenzao, Liao
dynasty. Xuanhua, Hebei
province.

in Clear Water the artist's hand follows the example of Huang Quan; the outline of the figures is very marked, at the expense of the lines inside it. Yet the arrangement of the figures is rather clumsy, although it does effectively convey the bustle of life in a marshy environment, where the arrival of a pair of waders puts a swarm of insects to flight. The birds are placed symmetrically opposite one another but distinguished by slight discrepancies: one, for example, is still placing a foot on the ground, the other flapping its wings. Higher up, more waders take to the air. The rest of the painting is filled with typical decorations: the ground under the waders' feet echoes on a tiny scale a landscape with pointed mountains, of the kind that we see so often in the frescoes at Dunhuang, but in a quite different location. In the Buddhist murals a module like this would have been used in the upper part of the composition, to create a sense of perspective; here, instead, the module has been adapted to represent the soil of the swamp. The clouds in the sky are represented without hesitation, in rapid brushstrokes in a standard, trefoil shape called *lingzhi*, or "mushroom of immortality."

23

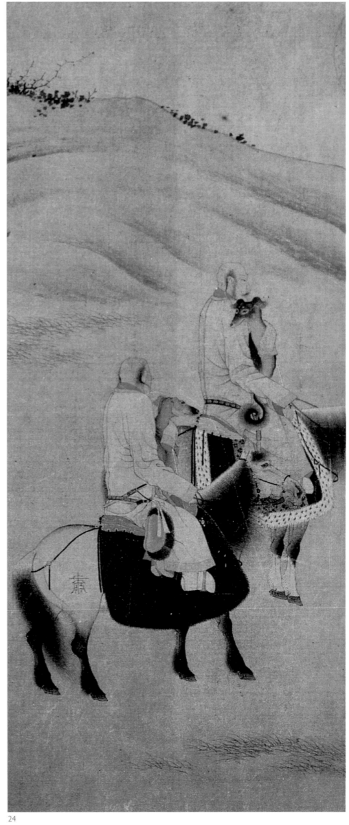

24

23. *Mating Cries in Clear Water*, mural on wood from the tomb of Jiefang Yingzi Liao, Liao dynasty.

24. Hu Gui, *Return from the Hunt (Huilietu)*, detail, beginning of 10th century CE. Taipei, National Palace Museum.

THE FACE OF DEATH

The same liveliness of clothing and individuality of features found in the murals of the Liao tombs has been handed down to us almost intact from life as well, thanks to the discovery in one tomb of a mummy with a death mask, a customary practice among the Khitan people. The dressing of the corpse, in mask and costume, appears to be a sort of preparation for eternity, for the life to come, in which the deceased had to present him or herself in the best possible condition. The mask of a Liao princess and her husband are the largest found so far in Inner Mongolia: the sheet of gold was beaten into shape on the face of the corpse, the eyes and eyebrows were engraved; a net of silver filigree gathered the man's hair, which followed the fashion of the time in being worn long and tied at the back.

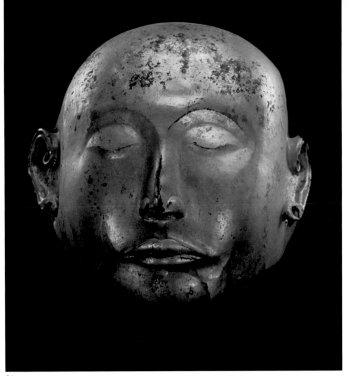

26

27

25. Facing page: Gold funerary mask, Liao dynasty, about 916-1125 CE. Inner Mongolia Institute of Cultural Relics and Archaeology, Hohhot, Inner Mongolia Autonomous Region.

26. Funerary mask, Liao dynasty, about 916-1125 CE.

27. Gold reliquary, Liao dynasty, about 916-1125 CE.

CHINESE ART

GOLD, INCENSE… AND POTTERY

In 1062 the dynasty financed the construction of a complex for the Buddhist Huayan sect in the capital Datong. It was not until the 16th century that the buildings were split into two units, the Lower Huayan Temple (Xia Huayansi), and the Upper Temple. Long before the monastery itself was built, the monks had decided to build a library where they could store the Scriptures of the Baojia Order. This was in 1038: the date is inscribed on a beam.

The desks in which the *sūtras* are housed constitute a masterpiece of joinery but what attracts the visitor's gaze is a magnificent pageant of terracotta statues. Each bodhisattva has an elongated bust; the folds of his robe are piled up on his knees; his throne, which stands on a tall pedestal, consists of a double lotus, with the stamens peeping out between the inner and outer row of petals. The expressions are all equally concentrated, conveying a sense of benevolent assurance; it is the extreme variety of the positions of the arms, always highly elegant, that gives the individual figures their personality.

The jewelry found in Liao tombs is in the same style as the metalwork of the last Tang, but who influenced whom? The Chinese had always preferred to import the exotic gold work of Central Asia, and the nomads had always been fascinated by the technology of Chinese ceramics. Non-sedentary people could hardly permit themselves the luxury of possessing a service in porcelain, which would have been unlikely to survive being carried around on their frequent moves. So while the Tang court had a passion for nomad jewelry, it is likely that Liao pottery had in its turn been influenced by the Chinese, especially the less elitist, more popular kind, with a simple yet striking decoration: Cizhou ware,

29

30

28. Facing page: Stoneware jug in the form of a mermaid, Liao dynasty, 10th-11th century CE. London, British Museum.

29. Ceramic statue of the Luohuan Tamrabhadra, Liao dynasty. Paris, Musée National des Arts Asiatiques-Guimet.

30. Gold objects, Liao dynasty, 10th-11th century CE.

coated with white slip. The potters who worked for the Khitan dynasty were in all probability Chinese craftsmen taken as hostages, or sent as gifts to the new rulers.

For example, the kilns in the district of Ding now served the Liao: a cup with a stamped decoration of children, flowers and auspicious symbols, covered with a white glaze, dates from the first half of the 11th century. The nomad patrons liked to see new forms in pottery: they were fascinated by motifs in the form of birds (such as a vase with neck and mouth that turn into the head of a bird) and by imitations of the leather containers to which the khans were more accustomed: potters even simulated the typical stitching and decorations used on leather and coated the pieces with a pale brown glaze. The Liao were also intrigued by the hybridization of forms, as is apparent from the stoneware jug in the shape of a mermaid that can be seen in the British Museum, a unique figure in the panorama of Chinese iconography.

The ceramicists of the 11th century were able to exercise better control over the melting of colored lead glazes. The sober forms of a simple ceramic bowl are enlivened by a splendid emerald green. It was in this period that they succeeded in keeping the glaze in "three-color" sancai pottery in the areas where they wanted it. This technological progress made it possible to conceive such a lifelike statue as the *Seated Luohan* (the word means a disciple of Buddha) in the Musée Guimet (Paris), which confirms the Liao genius for portraiture. It was probably part of a set of *luohans* (usually consisting of eight or sixteen figures, but sometimes made up of as many as five hundred), located in the Golden Hall of one of the many monasteries patronized by the Liao dynasty. The staring and somewhat squinting eyes, the open nostrils, the slightly curled upper lip: all combine to communicate the concentration of the figure and to impose a pause of silent reverence on the inattentive worshiper passing before it. *(S. B.)*

31

31. Porcelain bowl with green glaze, Liao dynasty, 11th century CE. Bath, Museum of East Asian Art.

32. Facing page: Porcelain bottle with brown glaze, in imitation of leather containers, Liao dynasty, 11th century CE. Bath, Museum of East Asian Art.

7. The Song Dynasty and the Apogee of Chinese Art

With the Song dynasty (960-1279) Chinese civilization was at the height of its power. The State maintained both a professional army and a formidable navy, maritime trade was prosperous, it was the highest producer of iron in the world at the time, and the capital, Kaifeng, boasted a highly sophisticated metropolitan culture. Nonetheless, the Song were unable to defend themselves when the Mongols invaded from the north and were eventually defeated.

In 960, a military coup brought the house of Song to power, with Taizu as emperor, soon to be succeeded by his younger brother, Taizong. Taizu gained power thanks to the might of his army, but once in power he made a bold decision, choosing to demilitarize the ruling class by keeping the generals in his entourage away from the political arena. This move is understandable, bearing in mind that for centuries the empire had been subjected to debilitating pressure on both its northern and eastern borders, chiefly from nomadic tribes.

And new enemies were looming to the north – one after the other, the Nüzhen, Dongxiang and Mongols all posed a threat to the Song. The maintenance of frontier garrisons was an expensive business and also constituted a threat, as power was concentrated in the hands of a few

1. Facing page: Portrait of Emperor Sung Taizu, detail, Northern Song dynasty, second half of 10th century CE.

2. Rectangular bronze mirror with engraved floral decoration, Southern Song dynasty, 12th century. Bath, Museum of East Asian Art.

3

3. Portrait of Empress Cao,
Song dynasty. New York,
Granger Collection.

generals. So a choice had to be made between the danger of a coup from within and keeping the external enemy at bay. Taizu therefore decided not to entrust the security of his own lineage to a warrior class. Following the same principle, at the beginning of the year 1000, the Chinese government responded to the pressure from the Khitan in the north by paying them tribute. However conciliatory this diplomatic policy might appear, it was a less expensive option for the government than funding garrisons in the north.

Another consideration was the fact that, once pacified, the Khitan (i.e. the Liao dynasty) became a prime source of custom for the goods produced by the Song. In the middle of the 11th century the Song defused the threat from the Western Xia in the same way (by paying them off in silver, silk, and tea). From the 11th century, the expansion of the empire took new directions, no longer looking to the north and northwest, but to the east and south. It was in this period, a kind of Pax Sinica, that the empire established itself as a great sea power. Navigators perfected the use of the compass, and pottery, tea, textiles, and metals (the last partly obtained by mining with explosives) were transported all over Southeast Asia in vessels up to 100 feet (30 meters) long. China imported ivory, spices, and most notably horses, which the Middle Kingdom had always had to source from territories not under its rule. Since trade to the north was erratic during this period because of guerrilla warfare with the nomads, horses were brought in from Thailand.

The population boomed, reaching 100 million and the prosperous times induced many peasants to move to urban areas, where the presence of these new city dwellers encouraged the development of services, the education system, and the publishing industry. People from the same area tended to specialize in the same sort of trade, so when

4

**4. Cizhou pottery headrest,
Song dynasty. Shanghai,
Shanghai Museum.**

5

5. Sculpture of arhat with
tiger, Northern Song
dynasty. Xi'an, Shaanxi
History Museum.

craftsmen migrated they organized themselves into guilds. Chinese craftsmen were much sought after for their skills from lands as far away as Central Asia, with the result that nomadic tribes would sometimes kidnap Chinese blacksmiths, goldsmiths, engravers, and weavers to make use of their skilled craftsmanship. In the south, the land began to be cultivated on an intensive level and money began to circulate widely. In the 12th century, the southern region of Yunnan, now part of the People's Republic of China, belonged to the kingdom of Dali. It was a region on the periphery in artistic terms, where the style of painting remained anchored to that of the Tang, but sculpture was subject to innovative influences from India. The real problem was that the new northern powers had broken the State's trade links with Central Asia. In the early decades of the 12th century, China experienced acute financial crisis; the land was in the hands of a few and tax evasion was common. It was no longer possible to maintain the old strategy of paying annual tributes, as the State coffers could not meet the strain. In 1115, the Song formed an alliance with the Nüzhen, situated even further to the north, aiming to defeat the Liao by closing them in the jaws of a pincer movement, attacking on two opposing fronts. Once victory had been won, the Nüzhen continued their movement south from their capital of Beijing (then Yanjing) to the Song capital, Kaifeng. In 1127, Huizong, a ruler with great artistic gifts and a patron of culture, was forced to kneel before the new enemy dynasty. He was taken as a hostage to the icy territories of the north, a place from which he would never return, an unbearable trauma for the Song courtiers. And so the Nüzhen created their Jin, or "Gold" dynasty.

6. Ceramic fish with human head, Northern Song dynasty, 11th century. Bath, Museum of East Asian Art.

THE JIN NOMADS AND THE PLASTIC ARTS

By the 12th century, the kilns in the north had fallen into the hands of the Nüzhen nomads, creating a new client base for ceramic ware, which in turn gave rise to new techniques. Demand was so great that Ding ceramists started using the stamping method to apply decoration to vases rather than engraving. They would also sometimes use iron oxide applied with a brush, the oxide turning copper-red when fired. Children playing games were a favourite decorative theme for the potters. The fascination of Jun ware on the other hand lay in the purity of its forms, and the colors of the glaze. Potters continued to spurn the use of any underglaze figurative decoration, as is evident from the Jun plate with a green glaze, where the surface seems to shimmer through the extensive crazing. A clear shift in taste can be discerned in the coloring of the slip: while glazes prior to the 12th century had earthy shades, they were

7

7. Ding dish with stamped
motif of camellias and
phoenixes, Jin dynasty,
late 12th century CE. Bath,
Museum of East Asian Art.

now characterized by "ethereal" tints. By now the potters were able to exercise perfect control over the running of the underglaze colors; the abstract smudging that had often been a result of chance and which had been so much in vogue during the Tang period, disappeared from Chinese pottery decoration. A fundamental technological innovation was introduced in the Cizhou pottery of the 13th century; overglaze pigments (in red, green and yellow) were used to decorate vases with figurative motifs, without firing. This technique of using enamels and *cloi-*sonné would be preferred by future dynasties, from the Ming onward. Since so much of the painting on scrolls has been lost – apart from "flowers and birds" and landscapes – we look to the decoration on pottery to provide us with a more complete range of pictorial themes than can be seen on the surviving paintings. The Jin, like the Liao, were generous patrons of Buddhist art. The northern monasteries have preserved a number of groups of terracotta statues, with some *luohans* reaching up to 3 feet or a meter in height, but there are few wooden

8

8. Jun plate with green glaze, from Henan, Jin dynasty. Bath, Museum of East Asian Art.

9

9. Cizhou pot decorated
with pigments applied
overglaze, Jin dynasty,
13th-14th century CE.
Toronto, Royal Ontario
Museum.

10. Facing page: Wooden
statue of the Buddha
Avalokiteśvara in *lilārāja*,
Jin dynasty, 11th-12th
century CE. London,
British Museum.

A CREATION OF THE MIND

"Landscape painting is a creation of the mind and is intrinsically superior art." So said Mi Fu, the dynasty's most versatile talent. Perhaps this is therefore a good point at which to examine Song landscape painting from the 10th century onward. It became an increasingly conceptual form of art, an abstraction of reality, with brushstrokes coming ever closer to those used in calligraphy, at a level which made the divide between professional painters and scholarly painters unbridgeable. The professional painters sought a realistic, vivid representation of the subject, which the Chinese call *xiesheng*, "transcribing from life," while the scholarly painters tried to capture the essence of the subject and a personal reaction to it, defining their approach as *xieyi*, "transcribing the idea." When seeking to "transcribe the idea," painters made no attempt to use perspective, which had long been a part of the Chinese visual heritage; the court carpenters made *jiehua*, "ruler-lined pictures" or scrolls that depicted architectural subjects in isometric perspective and with precise brushwork.

Until the Song dynasty, the looms used to make silk scrolls for painting had a maximum width of 23.6 in (60 cm). As a result, artists tended to paint on vertical hanging scrolls of this length, as each new scroll, with its different warp and weft, absorbed the ink in a different way. When scrolls were used horizontally, formed by joining different pieces of cloth together, painters tried to divide their pictures up correspondingly, to avoid sudden changes in the tone of the ink.

So landscape painting grew in popularity, although we know from literary sources that the human figure remained the most fashionable subject matter for painting. While over the centuries collectors have favored works that no longer reflect the taste of the 12th-13th century, the Song dynasty is fortunately the first for which we do not have to rely largely on copies to trace developments in painting.

The dynasts sought out certain *xiesheng* painters to attend the Yuhuayuan, the Imperial Academy of Painting, which had precedents at the court of Chengdu and at Nanjing. It functioned as a department of the Hanlin Yuan, the Academy of Examinations, and so admission was by selection. Candidates were assigned a theme, often an old poem, which produced interesting results when the key verse described a scent, or a feeling.

The originality of the idea was an important factor in selection of the candidates. Once admitted to the school, however, they were expected to achieve a formal resemblance to the object they were painting, so the academy ran the risk of becoming a center of hackneyed mannerism. It is worth giving a few statistics to point out just how small and very selective the academy was: on average there were just three tenured painters, six apprentice painters, four assistants, and forty students.

It should not be forgotten that those who were admitted to the Hanlin had access to the imperial collection. On the one hand this constituted a privilege and a precious opportunity for study, given that a catalog of the imperial paintings commissioned by Huizong ran to around 6000; on the other it made it harder not to fall into line with the taste of the wealthiest collector in the country, the emperor himself.

Guo Xi was born around 1020 at Wenxian, in Henan, in the northern part of the empire. An assistant professor at the Yuhuayuan, he was very prolific and was celebrated for the way he painted bare trees set in wintry landscapes. Shenzong liked his work, but not Huizong, who banished his paintings to a storeroom (an indication of Huizong's exacting, non-academic taste). His example was soon followed by other collectors

14

14. Example of *pingyuan* (level perspective), from a handbook of painting of the 17th century CE.

15

16

15. Guo Xi, *Early Spring*,
1072 CE, Northern Song
dynasty, 62.2x42.5 in
(158x108 cm). Taipei,
National Palace Museum.

16. Guo Xi, *Deep Valley*,
detail, Northern Song
dynasty. Shanghai,
Shanghai Museum.

anxious to keep up with fashion and it reached the point where one of Guo Xi's pictures was used as a rag by a restorer. Luckily a connoisseur realized what was happening in time and rescued the work. When commissioned to decorate the walls of the academy's rooms with murals, Guo had a brilliant idea: he asked the masons not to spread the plaster uniformly, but to create projections and hollows by applying it directly with their hands. He then used the undulations to paint elements of landscape, obtaining a remarkable impasto effect. His *Early Spring* is the first signed and dated (1072) painting in the history of Chinese art.

In terms of composition in the paintings that have been preserved, Guo accords the mass of a mountain a central position, where it seems animated by an inner energy, like a coiled snake.

His brushstrokes are longer, wetter and in general more complex than those of Fan Kuan and the variety in the arrangement of the picture's

17. Facing page: Fan Kuan, *Snowy Landscape*, Song dynasty. Tianji, Museum of Art.

18. Fan Guan (attrib.), *Seated Alone by a Stream*, Song dynasty, early 12th century CE.

19. Huizong, *Chaffinches and Bamboo*, detail, Song dynasty, 1100-25 CE. New York, Metropolitan Museum of Art.

different components, the way the different elements of mass are positioned, leads the eye through the painting. Guo was the first to use effects of highlighting for the mountain crests without worrying about determining a single source of light. Instead he chose the most interesting effect on each occasion, often in a quite arbitrary and inconsistent manner. In Guo Xi's works and in Chinese painting in general, light does not come from a point outside the picture; it is not an organizing principle "outside of things," perhaps because the Chinese did not believe in a creator of the universe; instead the light seems to issue from the objects themselves.

In 1110, Guo's son, Guo Si, collected his father's teachings in an essay (actually a miscellany, which probably includes the words of earlier masters), which he called *Linchuan Gaozhi* ("Lofty Aspirations Among Forests and Streams"). The master notes that to convey the depth of the scene, the painter has "three distances" at his disposal; *gaoyuan*, *shenyuan* and *pingyuan* (high, deep, and level perspective). Chinese painters had been using these perspectives since the 10th century, but it was Guo who brought them into focus in his manual.

Painting relied strongly on calligraphy; that painting developed out of calligraphy and then led back to it was deemed a good thing. The extraordinarily talented Su Shi was convinced of this. Born in 1036 at Meishan, in Sichuan, he would paint a bamboo plant in a single brushstroke, from ground upward to its tip. To friends who asked him why he didn't paint it in segments like everyone else, he replied; "Does bamboo grow in sections?" Some of his works have been preserved, but they can literally be counted on the fingers of one hand, and most of them depict branches of bamboo. He had an exclusive circle of friends, including the painter Wen Tong, whose death caused him much grief, and the calligrapher Huang Tingjian. They would meet and comment on the great artists of the past, often acted as examiners in state competitions, and discussed Taoism and Chan Buddhism, without ever straying from the path of orthodox Confucianism. They were intellectuals who had integrated into

20

21

234

20. Anonymous, *Stags among Red Maples*, late 10th century-early 11th century CE. Taipei, National Palace Museum.

21. Anonymous, *Peonies and Cat*, Song dynasty, 12th century CE.

the system perfectly and were careful not to question it. Nonetheless, Su Shi displeased the emperor and was exiled to Hainan for four years, an island with an extremely damp climate south of what is now Hong Kong. He died in 1101, on his way back to the capital from a second period in exile.

Mi Fu was a genius and a passionate admirer of a China of the earlier Jin and Tang eras. He was born in 1051 at Xiangyang, in Hubei, to a family from Shanxi. His mother was a lady in waiting to the wife of Emperor Renzong and a foreigner, of Sogdian origin. From an early age her son displayed a remarkable memory, quickly opening the way to a career as an official. His mother did everything she could to help him achieve his ambitions, but Mi Fu was his own worst enemy and was often moved from one post to another because he did not know how to compromise and keep his sharp tongue in check.

He was fanatical about cleanliness and collecting the works of calligraphers; before he became famous his mother was obliged to sell her

22   23

22. Wen Tong (1018/19-1079 CE), *Ink Bamboo*, Northern Song dynasty. Taipei, National Palace Museum.

23. Mi Fu (1052-1107 CE), *Fall Mountains and Propitious Pines*, mount in two colors, Northern Song dynasty.

24

24. Huizong (1082-1135 CE),
*Court Ladies Preparing
Newly Woven Silk*, detail,
Song dynasty, early
12th century CE. Boston,
Museum of Fine Arts.

own hairclips to fund his collecting mania. Mi Fu always kept a washbasin at his side (as the great Ni Zan was to do in the 14th century) without a towel, but only Mi Fu was allowed to use it.

If a visitor touched the paintings in his collection, he would clean them, eventually resorting to hiding the most valuable pieces from his visitors. He would also swap pieces when he grew tired of them. Even if they were not on display, he was content in the knowledge that he possessed examples of Jin or Tang calligraphy. He painted only on paper, untreated by alum, a very unforgiving medium which smudged easily and so constituted a real challenge to his skill as an artist. He also experimented with the use of sticks of paper or the lotus calyx to lay on the ink.

The subjects he depicted were given body and depth by the use of several coats of ink; he also employed a "pointillist" technique, by using many small, drop-shaped strokes, traditionally called *dian*, a technique that came to be known as *mi dian*, i.e. dots in the manner of Mi.

A favorite image and one that that recurred in his pictures was a mountain range wreathed in clouds, painted with the "boneless" technique. *Fall Mountains and Propitious Pines*, attributed to Mi, is a splendid example of this theme and very typical of his output: the *mi dian* texture suggests the softness of the covering of vegetation on the mountains, an effect the painter enhances by suffusing the peaks in light. In the foreground, at the bottom of the picture there is a shelter, inviting the viewer to "step into" the painting and view the wide sweep of its panorama from this point. *Fall Mountains and Propitious Pines* also illustrates the art of restoration, in which the painting is mounted on a panel of silk to protect it; the silk chosen by the recent restorers echoes the luminosity of the paper on which the picture is painted; its sober coloring, pale yellow and white, is not intrusive. Mi was also an excellent portraitist, especially of his favorite figures from the past. He collected his critical observations on the pieces in his own collection and on other masters in the *Huashi*

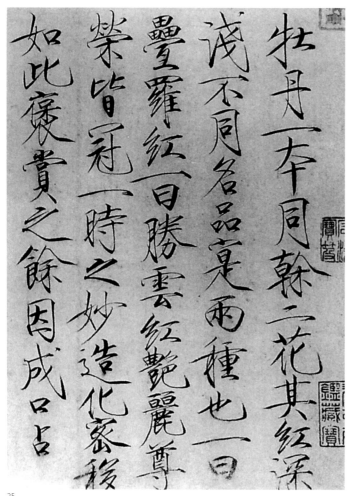

25

26

25. Huizong, *Poems and Peonies*, example of the script called "slender gold," Song dynasty, 1100-26 CE. Taipei, National Palace Museum.

26. *Emperor Huizong*, Song dynasty. Taipei, National Palace Museum.

("Account of Painting"). A great critic and historian of art, he did not simply repeat the judgments of earlier writers, but looked for himself, recording his own feelings and knowledge, without passing up the opportunity to promote outsiders and demolish the great. Unfortunately we cannot even be sure that any of the works attributed to him are actually original. He died in 1107 and so fate spared him from seeing the collapse of the Northern Song dynasty. Zhao Ji (1082-1135) was already an established master by the age of twenty. He painted in color and usually without the use of outlines. He favored flowers and birds as subject matter and liked to make paintings in fan shapes. These would then be copied by his courtiers, who pestered him to sign them. He held parties to show his portfolio; a kind of *vernissage* or opening night which members of the court were obliged attend. Zhao Ji invented his own style of calligraphy, the *jinshou* or "slender gold." It is an extremely elegant and fine style, elongated almost to the point of imbalance, but

pervaded by the powerful dynamism of a steady and gifted hand. There is no doubt that he possessed an extraordinary sensitivity to nature and his talent was also indisputable. This, combined with a bohemian attitude to life, serve to make him a fascinating subject, but part of his success was obviously due to the fact that he had ascended the imperial throne at an early age under the name of Huizong. If a picture painted at the Yuhuayuan was not to Huizong's liking, he would have it painted over with a coat of alum and the artist would then have to start over again, following his instructions. Zhao Ji also liked to create albums of the various species of flowers and animals that had been donated to the imperial garden. His output was so prolific and of such fine quality that we must hope that he had a studio of "ghost painters," and that his signature was a mark of approval rather than a declaration of authorship. Otherwise it has to be assumed that he devoted very little time to the art of government.

27

28

27. Huizong (1082-1135 CE), *The Five-Color Parakeet,* **Song dynasty. Boston, Museum of Fine Arts.**

28. Su Hanchen (attrib.), *Winter Play,* **Southern Song dynasty, 1130-60 CE. Taipei, National Palace Museum.**

THE OUTER ELEVATION AND THE INNER HEIGHT

The individualistic *xingshu* script, the "running" script, was employed in epistles and intimate journals in the Song dynasty. The 11th century produced the greatest masters of the age: Cai Xiang, Su Shi, Huang Tingjian, and Mi Fu. As we have seen, Mi Fu was also painter and a collector who sought out masterpieces to provide inspiration for his own calligraphy. In *Silk of Sichuan*, from 1088, he has used a "thirsty" brush, i. e. one dipped in not very dilute ink, and has sketched the characters with strong, confident strokes, not frightened to use a piece of silk that a collector might have kept to one side for decades, waiting for the strokes of a great calligrapher. The thickness of the strokes alternates – at times slight, at others forceful – in an enviably fluid rhythm. Huang Tingjian, a close friend of Su Shi, never painted. Born in 1045, he was a historian and aroused the wrath of some powerful individuals who sent him into exile more than once, as also happened to his friend. In exile in Sichuan he came across a work of calligraphy by the monk Huaisu, from the Tang period. It was a sudden inspiration and opened his eyes to calligraphy as a means of expressing one's feelings. In his *Poem in Seven Syllables*, Huang takes his reflection on the composition beyond the confines of the single character; he imbues the entire sheet with tension, using an irregular spacing between the lines, upsetting the balance at the beginning with characters of thicker strokes and recovering it in the middle and at the end with much more slender characters. In his inscriptions on pictures by other artists he often stressed that the most important thing to seek when painting was *yun*, resonance – or as the Italian poet Clemente Rebora would have put it, "the correspondence between the outer elevation / and the inner height." He died in 1105, at the age of seventy, four years after his inseparable friend Su Shi and two years before Mi Fu.

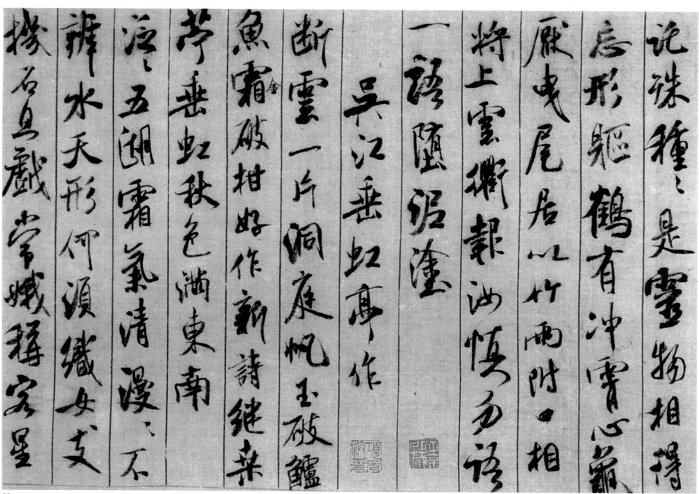

29

29. Mi Fu (1052-1107 CE),
Silk of Sichuan, **detail,**
Northern Song dynasty, 1088
CE. Taipei, National Palace
Museum.

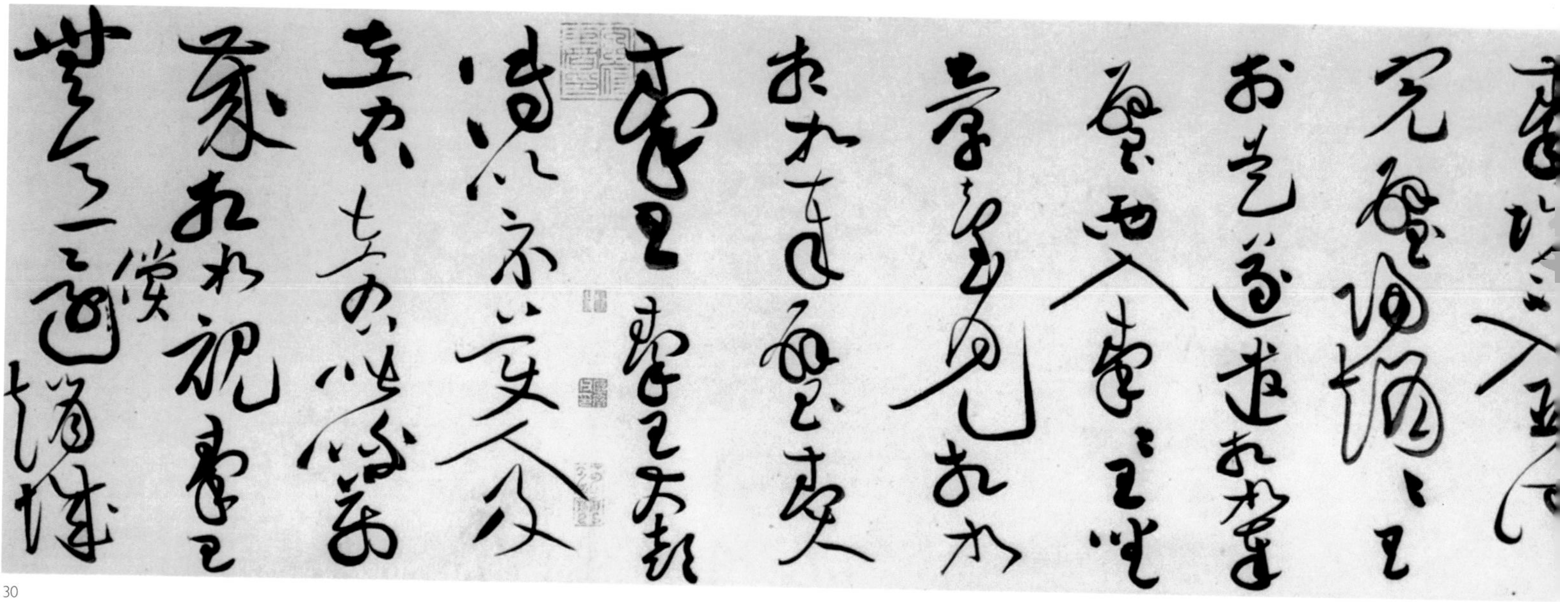

30

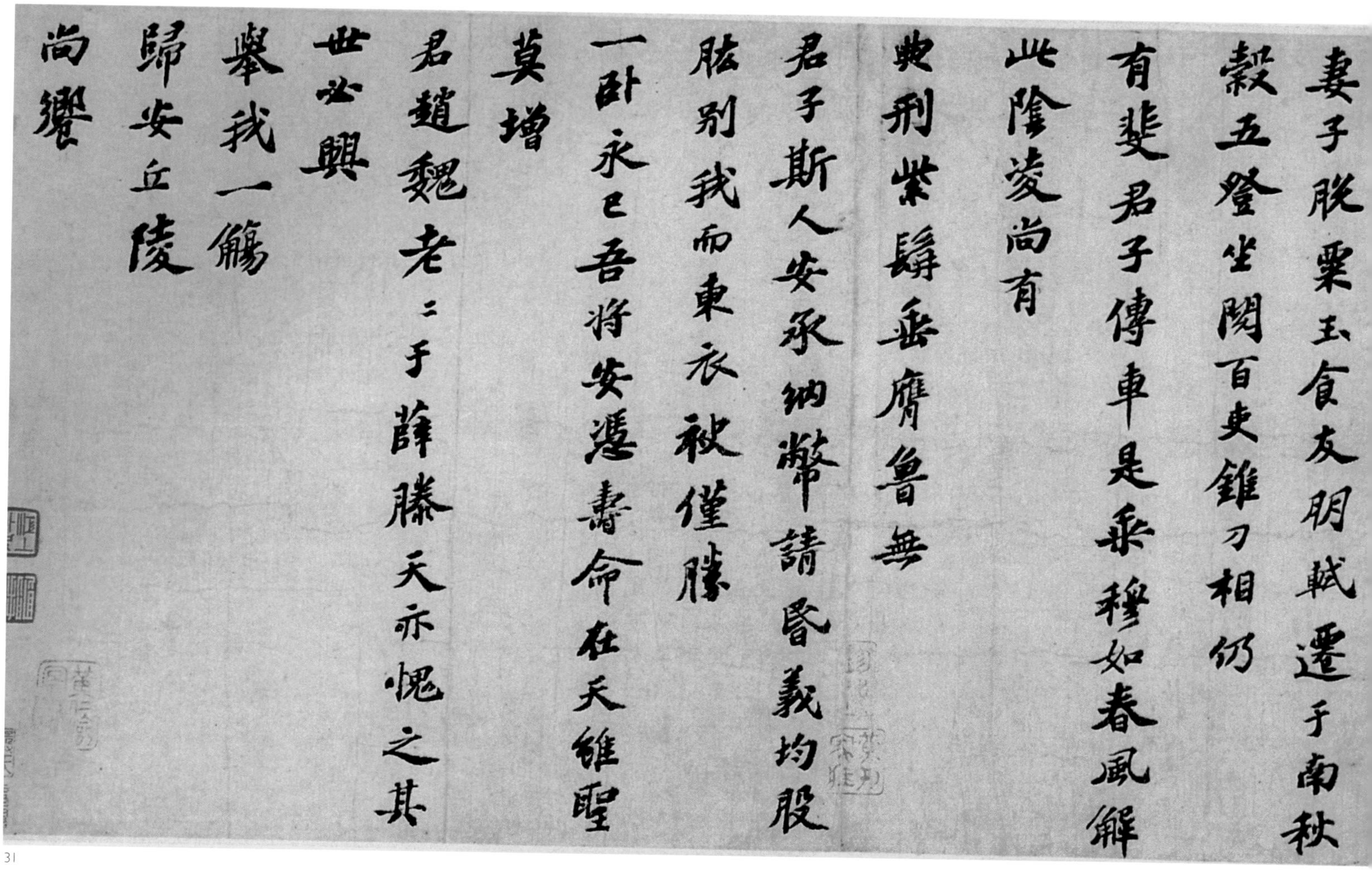

31

妻子脫粟玉食友明軾還于南秋
穀五登坐閣百吏錐刀相仍
有斐君子傳車是乘穆如春風觶
此陰夌尚有
蚑刑紫歸垂膺魯無
君子斯人安承納幣請醫義均股
肱別我而東衣袂僅縢
一卧永已吾將安憑壽命在天維聖
莫增
君趙魏老二于薛滕天亦愧之其
世必與
舉我一觴
歸安丘陵
尚饗

30. Huang Tingjian (1045-1105 CE), *Poem in Seven Syllables*, detail, Northern Song dynasty. Taipei, National Palace Museum.

31. Su Shi (1037-1101 CE), *Essay in Memory of Huang Jidao*, detail, Northern Song dynasty. Shanghai, Shanghai Museum.

SONG CERAMICS: DELIGHTING THE SENSE OF TOUCH

By the 11th century, the styles of the pottery produced by the kilns of the north and the south had begun to diverge. In the south Yue ware was admired and craftsmen began to make extremely elegant pots, with particularly slender, white bodies glazed in bluish shades, known as *qingbai*. The northern kilns also produced pottery with very slender walls called Ding ware; given its thinness, only shallow marks could be made in the clay and to prevent chipping it needed reinforcing at the lip with copper, gold or silver. Open forms (such as plates) were favored, along with ivory, cream and similar colors, with hints of brown, and of soy sauce. Potters in the district of Jun perfected the northern tradition of celadon stoneware. In this, a floral decoration was placed over a green glaze, or a thick light-blue, almost lavender glaze that grew thinner toward the edge, taking on an almost greenish-brown coloring and creating a silky, monochrome surface. Color and form helped to determine the "tactile" quality of the piece, in a combination that would make contemporary designers envious.

At a certain point, people began to grow tired of the monochrome – even though it seemed so commanding and complete that no further decoration was necessary, but the ceramists could only add abstract touches of color, or enliven the body of the vase with splashes of copper oxide.

The court monopolized the results of some experiments that were carried out in the kilns of the Jun district. They produced the very rare Ru ware, "for the court," with shapes of exquisite simplicity, an ash-colored body, lavender glaze and covered with very fine crazing; pieces were fired on spurs that left a slight mark on the base. The source of these pieces was unknown to modern experts, until archeologists found

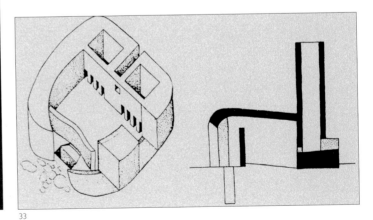

32

33

32. Jar with floral decorations, *qingbai* stoneware, Song dynasty, 10.5 in (26.6 cm).

33. Kilns at Yaozhou, Song dynasty. Beijing, Palace Museum.

34. Facing page: Yao *céladon* bowl with engraved peonies, Song dynasty, late 11th-early 12th century CE. Bath, Museum of East Asian Art.

about twenty examples in one loctation, at the kilns of Qingliangsi, in Baofeng county, Henan province. These were mostly pieces intended for the writing desks of the imperial family, so-called "gentleman's friends" such as pots for rinsing brushes.

The production of what is known as the Cizhou kiln was not in reality limited to a single kiln, but rather came from a widespread network of kilns, stretching from Shanxi to Shandong. They produced pottery for the common people, stoneware covered with cream slip (in imitation of the refined Ding ware) although decorated in highly imaginative ways. For example, the potters would apply two layers of slip in different colors and incise the upper layer to reveal the one below; most of the motifs were animals or flowers. Particularly charming, precisely because

of its simplicity, was the ware covered with dark slip, used chiefly in the tea ceremony, as we shall see in the southern continuation of the dynasty.

The coloring created by ceramists for Chaiyao ware was truly astonishing; a blue "like the sky after rain," over which were laid blotches of copper oxide that turned crimson and purple on firing.

In 1127, when the court was moved south, some of the pottery produced in the northern kilns would become the prerogative of the Jin and would no longer be generally available; production of the beautiful Ru ware, for instance, came to an abrupt halt, and was thus limited, more or less, to the years 1080-1100. The court was obliged to come up with new canons of taste, based on the products at its disposal.

35

35. Ru tripod vase, Song dynasty. Beijing, Palace Museum.

36. Cizhou ware, Northern
Song dynasty, 11th
century CE. Bath, Museum
of East Asian Art.

(on the back) and image (on the front), realizing what had been the Tang ideal of the *sanjue*, the three perfections. In a single work of art observers could consider the artist's handwriting (most important, given that calligraphy is the highest art in Chinese eyes), enjoy the poem, and finally let their gaze roam over the picture, judging whether it was a mere illustration or served as a complement or contrast to the sentiments expressed by the poetry. The three components can be — and often are — made by different artists, sometimes living centuries apart, such as a poem from the 4th century CE, inscribed by a calligrapher friend of the painter who has chosen to illustrate it: the three artists meet together in the smallest of spaces. The court retreated from the landscape to the microcosm of the garden. Flowers were always shown as being perfect in paintings; they were never represented as withered, since reality was already deemed to be wretched and impoverished enough.

Li Tang (born at Heyang, who lived around 1070-1150) experienced the transition from the Northern to the Southern Song in full. At around the age of seventy, he was given the highly responsible postion of being the first director of the reorganized academy of painting, under Gaozong. Li Tang organized his compositions into perfect alternations of space and mass; when painting he squeezed or even tapped the brush against the silk, developing the "axe-cut" stroke. This way of laying on the ink, sometimes almost in drips, gave forms a sense of solidity, an almost metallic property. In addition to landscapes, he painted portraits and pictures of buffalos.

In the scroll *Duke Wen of Jin Recovering His State*, over 27 feet (8 meters) long, Li's painting is characterized by a strong vein of narrative, borrowing devices from so-called "ruler-lined painting" (notable in the representation of the balustrade, in isometric perspective) and from theatrical scenery. The movement of the figures is concealed but is suggested by an enclosure of cloth, like the curtain of a theater, leading the eye from right to left and then right again, from the outside to the inside. It tells a story set in the 7th century BCE: the duke of Jin travels to China to pay a visit to other governors, in a sequence of six meetings. In each scene the building in which the meeting takes place is depicted from a different perspective; the articulation of the space suggests the passing of time. In the first illustration, one of the governors is receiving the duke of Jin while a team of horses is led into the courtyard as a gift.

Li Tang met his favorite and most talented pupil in a rather unusual manner. As the court fled from Kaifeng to Hangzhou, the master, like many others, hid in the woods to seek refuge from the nomadic invaders. While he rested, someone tried to steal his knapsack although it contained nothing but chalk and brushes. The robber was subsequently

40

248

40. Li Tang, *Itinerant Doctor*, detail, Southern Song dynasty. New York, Granger Collection.

41

41. Li Tang, *Soughing Winds among the Pines*, Southern Song dynasty, 1124 CE. Taipei, National Palace Museum.

42

43

42-43. Li Tang, *Duke Wen of Jin Recovering His State*, details of the scene of the gift of horses and the scene of the departure from the state of Chu, Southern Song dynasty, about 1140 CE. New York, Metropolitan Museum of Art.

caught and became his disciple, Xiao Zhao. It was Li Tang who ushered in the approach to landscape painting that would come to be known as the "Ma-Xia school," after the surnames of two of his pupils. He died after spending ten years in charge of the academy, while the much younger Ma Yuan and Xia Gui, were able to take his ideas further after his death. Liang Kai's career was a curious one. Starting out as a *baimiao* portraitist, depicting Buddhist and Taoist figures in a hyperrealistic style with sharp, vigorous outlines, he then gradually shifted to the monochrome ink of Chan inspiration. Ling eventually lost all interest in the academy, to the point of hanging up his Golden Belt – the highest honor a painter could receive – on a nail in a wall at the Yuhuayuan. Liang was skilled at capturing the essence of his subjects in their expressions, deftly portraying their concentration on and relationship with the objects of their attention. He painted with oblique strokes (from top to bottom and left to right, the *na* stroke; and from top to bottom and right to left, the *pie* stroke); as the ancients would have said, his brushstrokes recalled "broken reeds." Liang's surviving works are "abbreviated" paintings, *jianbi*, executed with just a few essential strokes; the superficial and extraneous have no place in his paintings. His works were highly appreciated by Japanese collectors in the Ashikaga period (14th-16th century). Mi Youren followed in the family tradition, being the son of Mi Fu. While Mi Fu had been a typical exponent of the Northern Song milieu, born in 1085, Mi Youren was active at the court of the Southern Song and died in 1165. Unlike his difficult father, he was able to win the emperor's favor and became a successful official. He continued to paint his father's characteristic subject matter, vistas of mountains lost in the clouds, showing great skill in the alternation of dilute and dense ink. The Mi were not the only family of artists, Ma Yuan was also descended from a line of painters and under Emperor Ningzong was awarded the Golden Belt at the academy. He is famous for having utilized a new, notably one-sided, "angled" composition; in two of the pictures reproduced here an intellectual is shown in the foreground, while his *alter ego* contemplates the landscape from one corner. The point of view is low, the distant mountains are flattened, while the ones close to are high. The brushwork is highly reminiscent of his master, Li Tang. Unlike many earlier landscape painters, he does not lose himself in detail, but dispenses with the extraneous, only bringing into play elements that create lines of force in the composition. In this manner, the observer's gaze is not allowed to linger in the scene, but is led where the artist wants to take it. The painter suggests a correspondence between the void he has created and the silence that descends on a person contemplating nature. However, Ma Yuan did not stick exclusively to the angled composition. We have cop-

44

44. Liang Kai, *Sage*, mount in two colors, Southern Song dynasty, 1140-1210 CE, 19.2x10.9 in (48.7x27.6 cm). Taipei, National Palace Museum.

ies of his wall paintings of vertical landscapes, which are striking in their power and yet are not at an angle. A comparison between two of his works with a similar composition illustrates this.

In *Viewing Plum Blossoms by Moonlight*, the official depicted in the scene is looking up and even the tree seems to be reaching for the moon. The servant, holding his master's lute, learns from him to be patient in contemplation of the landscape.

In *Scholar Viewing a Waterfall*, the figure is now looking downward, the

pine tree is also drooping, without any vigor. We do not see what the scholar is contemplating, it is not shared with us. The servant waits in embarrassment; he seems to sense his master's sadness. Ma Yuan creates an interplay of glances, prompting us to identify with the gaze of the servant, who is in turn observing the official, but he does not invite us to identify ourselves directly with him. The effect is a sensation of despondency, and of the artist's isolation, emotions that probably went hand in hand with the decline of the dynasty. Temüjin, leader of the

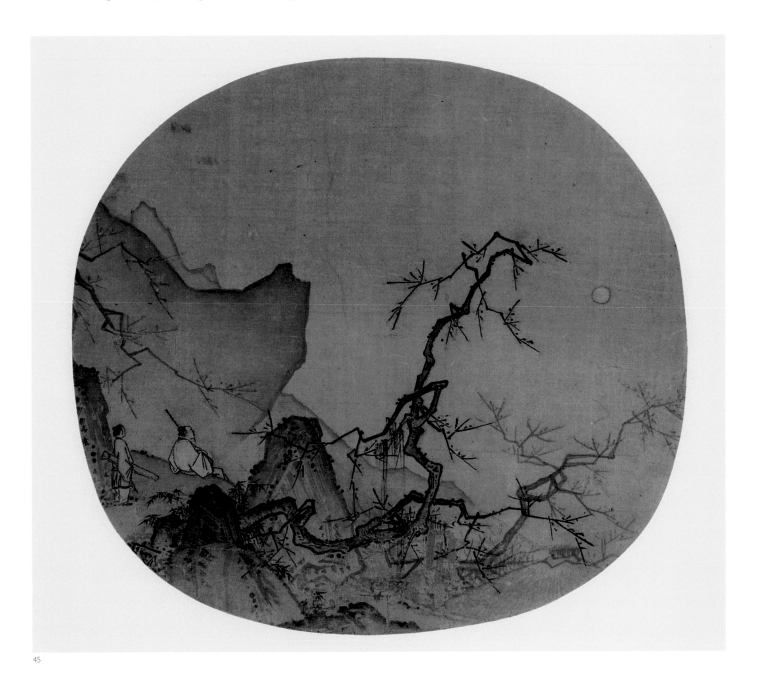

45

45. Ma Yuan, *Viewing Plum Blossoms by Moonlight*, fan mounted as an album leaf, Southern Song dynasty, 9.9x10.5 in (25.1x26.7 cm). New York, Metropolitan Museum of Art.

46. Facing page: Ma Yuan (flourished about 1190-1225 CE), *Scholar Viewing a Waterfall*, album leaf, detail, Southern Song dynasty, 9.8x10.2 in (24.9x26 cm). New York, Metropolitan Museum of Art.

47. Ma Yuan (flourished about 1190-1225 CE), *Bare Willows and Distant Mountains*, Southern Song dynasty. Boston, Museum of Fine Arts.

48

48. Ma Lin, *Waiting for Guests by Lamplight,* Southern Song dynasty. New York, Granger Collection.

Mongols, was already at large in the northern lands and was to go down in history under the name by which he became better known, Genghis Khan. With Ma Lin, who lived in the first half of the 13th century, we are again dealing with a family tradition – in this case he was the son of Ma Yuan and in all probability the two worked in the same studio. Ma Yuan had a number of apprentices and one malicious anecdote claims that he signed some of his son's best paintings in order to help him along in his career. In reality it would have been difficult for Ma Lin to surpass his father's talent as a landscape painter, but it was in the depiction of the domestic world that he showed himself to be a genuine poet. Ma Lin's *Waiting for Guests by Lamplight* portrays a scene of touching simplicity: a gathering of friends to admire the plum blossom under the light of the full moon. The painting does not even focus on the moment of the contemplation of nature, moving in itself, but on the anxious wait for companions with whom to share this joy. Despite the passing of the centuries, this masterly depiction of friendship and the small things of life

still has a powerful impact. In the superb *Layer upon Layer of Icy Silk*, Ma Lin confirms his predilection for an absolute refinement of composition, helping us to perceive the crisp cold of the first blossoming; our gaze lingers on the silent space prepared for the poem composed by the empress Yang Meizi (1162-1232), who had also inscribed works by his father. When he was a boy Li Song, who also lived during the first half of the 13th century, worked as a carpenter, but was then adopted by the painter Li Congxun. He never forgot his humble origins, but rather took inspiration from them for his groups of figures. What emerges is his capacity to immerse himself in the reality of the common people, interpreting their anxieties and fleeting moments of happiness. This is rare in Chinese painting, which usually remains intellectual and courtly and does not look beyond the milieu of the aristocracy. It is perhaps for this reason that paintings of popular subjects (the fangsuhua, genre scenes) are even more surprising. Li's picture *Peddler of Knickknacks* gives him an opportunity to build up detail with meticulous, almost finicky brush-

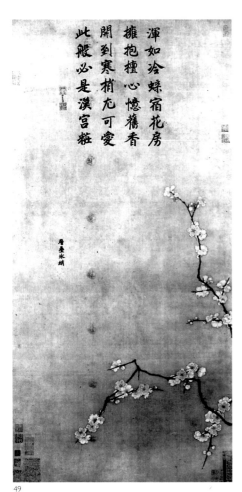

49

50

49. Ma Lin, *Layer upon Layer of Icy Silk*, Southern Song dynasty, 39.8x19.5 in (101x49.6 cm). Beijing, Palace Museum.

50. Ma Lin, *Landscape with Large Pine*, Southern Song dynasty, about 1250 CE. New York, Metropolitan Museum of Art.

51

51. Ma Lin, *Orchids*,
Southern Song dynasty,
13th century CE, 10.3x8.8 in
(26.2x22.4 cm). New York,
Metropolitan Museum
of Art.

work. The public was particularly fond of Chen Rong's dragons, as is evident from *Nine Dragons*, a scroll 36 feet (11 meters) long, painted in 1244 and scattered with around 50 inscriptions and seals added by collectors and admirers. Chen's method of working was totally unorthodox. The first, and apparently indispensable step was to get drunk. He then painted clouds by splashing on ink (*pomo*), while the impression of the steam given off on the appearance of the dragons was obtained by spitting water onto the scroll. But that was not all. He even went so far as to use his hat as a pad with which to apply the ink. Only when he reached this point did he finally apply the finishing touches with the brush. He was even more audacious in his composition, where he made use of a metonymic technique, sometimes simply using a shoulder or a part of the head to suggest the entire dragon. Despite his apparent waywardness, this Jackson Pollock of the 13th century was obviously good at reconciling pleasure with duty, since he carried out his job as a government official without a hint of reproach.

52

52. Li Song, *Peddler of Knickknacks*, Southern Song dynasty, 1211 CE, 10x27.8 in (25.5x70.5 cm). Beijing, Palace Museum.

53

53. Chen Rong (1235-1262),
Nine Dragons, detail,
Southern Song dynasty,
1244 CE, 18.2x431.7 in
(46.3x1096.4 cm). Boston,
Museum of Fine Arts.

THE CLAY CHANGES, AND WITH IT THE POTTERY

Under the Song dynasty, the production of high quality pottery grew more widespread. It was no longer possible to identify pieces as being from one of just a few kilns with a monopoly on the technology; all of them shared a very high level of expertise. The green shade of the slip used for celadon, for example, became more uniform throughout the northern territory. It was only under the Song that ceramics came to be preferred over precious metals, probably because of the emphasis placed on a quiet discretion in taste by the scholar-officials. Unfortunately Chinese pottery is steeped in anonymity, we do not even know

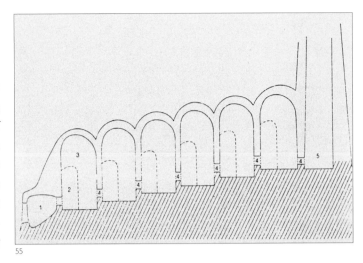

55

CHINESE ART

56

54. Facing page: Guan vase, Southern Song dynasty, 12th-13th century. London, British Museum.

55. Diagram of a dragon kiln at Longquan for the firing of pottery, Southern Song dynasty.

56. Jizhou ware, cup with leaf decoration, Southern Song dynasty, late 12th century CE. Bath, Museum of East Asian Art.

the name of one single potter. There was a boom in production during the course of the Song dynasty, thanks to the invention of "dragon kilns" that exploited natural slopes to cover a distance of many yards, and could hold as many as 20,000 pieces at a time.

The kilns for the new capital, in the vicinity of Hangzhou, produced slender-walled *guan*, "imperial," ware from a clay blend that turned dark when fired, while the body was coated with gray-blue glaze. In practice Guan ware was a version of the products from the Ru kilns produced "in exile"; potters had tried to reproduce them, but the blend of clays was not the same. The slip came out thicker and paler, the crazing more dense. In a reaction both to the failure of diplomatic negotiations with the nomads and the flourishing archeological excavations, the elite came to appreciate more conservative forms, echoing the styles of past dynasties.

The *qingbai* porcelain (with characteristics already mentioned: thin, white walls, a blue-tinted slip of irregular thickness) produced at Jingdezhen contain motifs so similar to those of the Ding ware of the Northern Song period that it is suspected to be the work of northern craftsmen who had fled at the approach of the Jin. The decoration of Jian ware responded promptly to the new requirements of the tea ceremony. The preparation of tea had become an inescapable ritual for high society – Emperor Huizong had even gone to the trouble of writing a book of tea etiquette, the *Da Guan Cha Lun* ("Treatise on Tea") – and potters were now asked for dark cups to set off the ever-changing iridescence of the beverage. The ceramists increased the oiliness of the slip by adding iron; the ripple effect on the surface of the tea could be enhanced by decorating the bottom of the cup with a "hare's-fur" pattern. Fujian, the province in South China opposite the island of Taiwan, produced teacups with a dark green slip specifically for export to Japan.

The stoneware cup from Jizhou in the illustration, is a splendid example of the ingenuity with which potters sought to amaze their clients. In this piece a leaf has been placed between the body of the pot and the slip; when the cup was fired in the kiln the leaf burned away, leaving behind its impression in the glaze. As the drinker slowly sips his tea, this elegant decoration on the bottom of the cup is revealed progres-

57

**57. Longquan ware, teacup,
Southern Song dynasty,
late 12th-early 13th century
CE. Bath, Museum of East
Asian Art.**

58

sively, brought to life by its continual interaction with the drink.

The tradition of celadon ware, pottery with a green glaze, was maintained. In the south the kilns of Longquan set out to imitate Guan ware, but in the north the production of the Yaozhou kiln (in Shaanxi) made no attempt at imitation, instead the pieces were decorated with more rapid incisions.

The Longquan kilns applied a jade green slip of dazzling purity, on a reddish-brown body. The monochrome solidity of the pieces is rendered more lively by dense crazing, rarely by figurative decoration.

When they did decorate Longquan ware, the Song potters mostly used incisions, in the tradition of Yao ware. The preference of the Northern Song had been for Longquan vases with thin walls and thick glaze (in a yellowish-green color, sometimes with engraved decorations); now the Southern Song favored a thick body and thin glaze (plum green). The attraction of Jizhou ware lay purely in the inventiveness of the decoration, and for this reason it pleased the Jin and the Yuan, the northern dynasties of nomad origin. But now we are already talking about the taste of the 14th century.

CHINESE ART

265

58. Cizhou kiln, cup decorated with phoenixes, Southern Song dynasty, 13th century CE. Bath, Museum of East Asian Art. The phoenix **motifs were created by the application of paper figurines: during the firing the figurines burned away, leaving their impression behind.**

CARVED SILK

The Song perfected the art of lacquer, adding ash or clay to the resin, to make a more malleable lacquer which could then be painted onto objects made of wood. The lacquer ensured that objects such as trays, cup-stands for the tea ceremony, and other furniture would be strong but light; decoration such as Buddhist symbols could also be carved into the lacquer. Wenzhou was one of the most advanced centers for laqueur ware. The lacquer was either used as a monochrome, or was laid on in several layers of different colors so that the surface of the piece could be cut away to reveal the color of the layer beneath, in much the same way as in Jizhou pottery. Alternatively the lacquer was inlaid with mother of pearl, or gold dust was mixed with the resin to make the piece look more brilliant, producing colors that changed under the light. An elegant silver box from the 13th century, engraved and decorated with niello (inlaid with a black metallic alloy), displays the same decorative motifs as were used in lacquer ware. Scenes of flowers and birds, so fashionable in 12th- and 13th-century painting, were drawn not just in ink, but were created using silk too. Thanks to a special device installed on a loom, the warp and weft threads were kept slightly apart so that the images created under the nimble figures of the weavers appeared to stand out. This technique is known as "carved silk," or kesi, and was already in use in Central Asia during the Tang period, but became more highly developed under the Song. It was used to decorate the surface of the more "stylish" of everyday objects, such as tapestries, clothing, and shoes. In their separate quarters, noblewomen would depict the same subjects as the painters of the time, but in kesi. Women were not precluded from painting. If anything, it was the other way round and men were loath to try their hand at producing kesi on the loom. The 12th-century artist, Zhu Kerou, was acknowledged as the most refined exponent of kesi; her images of peonies were unrivalled.

59

59. Silver box with engraved and nielloed decoration, Southern Song dynasty, 13th century CE. Bath, Museum of East Asian Art.

60. Zhu Kerou, *Peonies,*
kesi tapestry, Southern
Song dynasty, 13th
century CE. Shenyang,
Liaoning Provincial
Museum.

SPECIAL FOCUS

HEAVEN AND HELL AT DAZU

In the luxuriant countryside of Sichuan, at a vast site called Dazu, Buddhist temples had been carved into the rock ever since the Tang period, just as at Dunhuang or Longmen. Toward the end of the 12th century, after making a long journey through the region for study purposes, Zhao Zhifeng, a fervent follower of Buddhism, returned to the place of his birth and decided to create a complex of statues dedicated to Tantric Buddhism. The place Zhao had in mind was on the hill of Baodingshan, close to where he had spent his childhood. It was a natural am-

phitheater, ideal for presenting what would be a kind of visual catechism, a sequence of statues arranged in a U-shape. Zhao Zhifeng was untiring in raising funds for the work. He had been studying Tantric Buddhism since the age of five, and was just nineteen when he embarked on this project. It took the stonemasons seventy years (from 1179 to 1249) to complete Zhao's ambitious plan. The pilgrims who flocked there found the slope of the hill lined with an extraordinary procession of images, suggesting a route to be followed by the spirit.

268

1-II. The Nirvāna of the
Buddha, general view
and detail of the female
disciples of Shakyamuni,
12th-13th century CE.
Dazu, Sichuan.

II

The faithful must have been overawed by the divine figures that the sculptors portrayed with such dynamism, vigor, and personality. Visiting Dazu now, we linger in front of a temple steeped in gloom, where bodhisattvas delight in putting questions of doctrine to the Buddha; a little further on a huge triad looms some 26 feet (8 meters) tall, with Vairocana, Samantabhadra, Mañjuśri, the Buddha and the typical bodhisattvas of the Huayan sect carved out of a sheer slab of rock; next to them, a gilded Avalokiteśvara in his thousand-armed form is seated under a canopy. As soon as we emerge, reeling from the scale and grandeur of the statues, our way is blocked by a Buddha in Nirvana, almost 100 feet (30 meters) long.

The hill teems with images in high relief: episodes from the Great Peacock Sūtra, much venerated by Zhao Zhifeng's school; the Wheel of Rebirth, showing in a single, powerful mandala — a circle divided into six segments — the Buddhist cosmogram with all the creatures (gods, demons, men and animals) of the Tantric vision of the world.

On the northern wall, the Buddha Vairocana is frozen in the act of preaching. His teaching is represented in four groups of sculptures: the Buddha explains the importance of the self-sacrifice of parents for their children, recounts twenty episodes of the filial devotion displayed by the Buddha Shakyamuni in his previous incarnations, describes the paradise of Amitābha, and finally terrifies his audience by rattling off the various, terrible torments that await sinners in hell. When the pilgrims, impressed and dismayed, finally made their way out of the gully, they would certainly have had the impression, as Dante put it, of emerging "to see again the stars." *(S. B.)*

8. China under Foreign Rule: the Yuan Dynasty

Khanbaliq, the "city of the Khans" was the name by which Beijing was known to travelers in the 14th century, wherever they came from. Not all were merchants: a Franciscan missionary, Giovanni da Montecorvino, even lived there, the first archbishop of the city. Beijing was the political epicenter of an empire that stretched from Korea to the Dnieper River and of a people that had terrified Poland and Hungary. However, this empire was not Chinese, but Mongol, whose most famous leaders, Genghis Khan and his grandson Kublai, ruled during the first and second half of the thirteenth century respectively. The Chinese name of their dynasty was Yuan (1276-1368). Fourteenth-century China may have amazed the numerous foreign merchants that traversed its territory, but it was certainly no "land of Cockaigne" for its natives.

1. Facing page: Liu Kuan-tao, *Kublai Khan Hunting*, detail, Yuan dynasty, about 1280. Taipei, National Palace Museum.

2. Gilded statue of monk with begging bowl, detail, Yuan dynasty, 14th century. Taipei, National Palace Museum.

MONGOL DOMINATION AND INDIGENOUS REBELLION

Yuan society suffered a great inequality in taxation; the Mongol civil and military elite was exempt from paying taxes, as were the clergy, especially the Buddhist priests, and the *semuren*, the "colored-eye people," i.e. foreign traders and tax collectors – Uighurs, Turks, Persians, Syrians, Tibetans, Russians, Venetians, Genoese – who took advantage of their privileges to practice usury.

As a result, the tax burden, linked to the amount of land in the individual's possession, fell on the common people and on medium to small landowners.

In addition the Mongols required people to carry out unpaid labor. The wealthiest landowners could escape this imposition by paying a sum of money; those who worked small and medium-sized farms, however, along with artisans, were periodically obliged to swell the ranks of the laborers employed on improvements to the irrigation system, in massive construction programs – always to the benefit of the ruling elite – or in shipyards building vessels for the transport of rice. The population was not happy with the employment of tax collectors of Persian or Central Asian origin nor with the transport and fiscal concessions from which foreign merchants benefited, to the detriment of the indigenous mercantile class. Under the Mongols, banknotes came into use; at that point the copper no longer used for cash was channeled largely into ornaments for Buddhist temples. Speculation by non-Chinese intermediaries triggered high inflation, and the condition of the masses was made even worse by the famine of 1325 and the floods of 1351.

Many intellectuals chose not to collaborate; some withdrew to hermitages in the mountains, others fled to Japan or returned to managing family estates. In order to quash any attempt at rebellion, the Mongols forbade the Han even to possess arms. However, the resistance of the common people was soon channeled into secret societies such as the White Lotuses, the Red Turbans and the White Clouds, placed under the protection of Amitābha or Maitreya. The population began to voice its discontent in a mass tax revolt. We can sympathize with the despairing complaint of the painter Ni Zan, when he declared "Paying taxes is ruinous [...] / I feel shackled to my rage / I think of abandoning my fields / I gather up my clothes and take to the hills at night." Within thirty years, the Mongol empire, now divided into satrapies or small provinces that communicated little with one another, disintegrated before the burgeoning organization

4

of resistance movements. The rebel leader Zhang Shicheng, a former trader in salt, took first Suzhou and then Hangzhou and the surrounding region of Jiangnan, the richest in the empire. In 1363 he had enough money to cast off the vassal's cloak and free himself from the Mongol yoke. He had long been assembling a court of intellectuals and artists that could add brilliance to his influence. Five years later the Ming, or "Bright" dynasty would be founded.

6

7

5. Facing page: *The Khan's Court*, from the manuscript *Jāmiʿ al-Tawārīkh* by Rashid al-Dīn, Yuan dynasty, about 1330. Berlin, Staatsbibliothek.

6. Xie Chufang, *Fascination of Nature*, Yuan dynasty, 1321. London, British Museum.

7. *Fish among Bamboo Canes*, Yuan dynasty. New York, Granger Collection.

NEW AIR FROM THE NORTH

The Song dynasty left the artists of the 14th century with the legacy of an affected mannerism. Some painters prided themselves on keeping the 13th-century tradition artificially alive, aiming to please particular patrons slow to embrace new tendencies, in part due to their need to disguise their position as *nouveaux riches* by adopting the taste of the ruling class of the preceding period.

A handful of brilliant artists decided instead to take a step further back, to the art of the Eastern Jin and the Tang, in order to start afresh

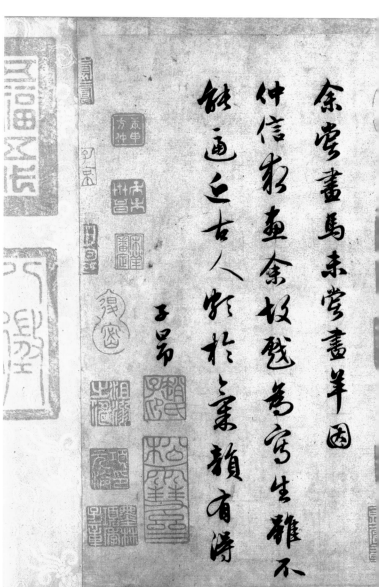

8. Zhao Mengfu, *Portrait of the Poet and Painter Su Shi*, Yuan dynasty. New York, Granger Collection.

9. Zhao Mengfu, *Sheep and Goat*, Yuan dynasty. Washington, Freer Gallery of Art, Smithsonian Institution.

and develop new solutions. The initiator of this key trend is thought to have been Xianyu Shu (1257-1302), an artist of northern, non-Chinese origin who brought a welcome breath of fresh air to connoisseurs weary of Song mannerism.

Xianyu Shu frequented the house of a very wealthy patron, Zhou Mi (1232-98), where he had the opportunity to examine two superb works of art: the *Treatise on Calligraphy* by Sun Guoting (second half of 7th century), a classic of the *xingli* script in the manner of Wang Xizhi, and the *Draft of a Eulogy for a Nephew* by Yan Zhenqing (709-785), an obligatory point of reference for anyone wishing to practice

the *xingshu* in vogue under the Tang. Xianyu encouraged Zhao Mengfu (1254-1322) to study the stelae of the Northern Wei and the manuscripts of the Tang. Historians of the art of the later dynasties do not hold the figure of Zhao Mengfu in great esteem, finding it difficult to ignore his collaboration with the Mongol elite; this represented an even graver fault in that Zhao was descended from a cadet branch of the Song imperial family and in this role could have made himself a champion of the people's desire for revolt.

Zhao was born in 1254 at Huzhou, in Zhejiang. In 1286 he was summoned to court by Emperor Shizu, better known as Kublai Khan.

After Shizu, he painted in the service of four more Mongol emperors, dying in 1322. In his career, he alternated his artistic calling (as director of the Hanlin Academy) with his administrative skills (as governor of Jiangxi and Zhejiang). Thanks to his status he was able to study various collections around the empire, even in the south.

In an inscription of 1301, written in his rather hypnotic script, slanting slightly to the right, Zhao revealed that for him "the most important thing is the antique spirit [guyi]." By "antique" he probably meant the dynasties of the Wei, Jin and Tang, completely sidestepping — as the greatest Yuan masters of the next generation were to do — the Song

10

278

10. Zhao Mengfu, *Horse and Groom in Winter*, Yuan dynasty. Taipei, National Palace Museum.

tradition. He may have made a few exceptions. There is a story that a painting by the great Mi Fu, who had lived two centuries before, was given to Zhao for restoration. He studied the scroll, took up his brush, approached the picture and then stopped, commenting; "I cannot restore it. I'm not equal to the task."

To Zhao the works of art of the Jin (not the nomads of the 12th century, but the imperial house of the 4th century CE) and the Tang were a model of the simple expression and frugal means that provided the best conditions for interpreting nature, the subject of his scrolls. In reality Zhao Mengfu's work surprises us by its diversity – he

hardly ever repeated himself. He even used to amuse himself with his friends by transforming blots of ink into a rock or a tree with a few brushstrokes.

Admittedly, the Yuan painters joined forces to shun the Song style. However, they did appreciate the perception of space shown by artists of the previous dynasty. Their paintings of the landscape had evolved decisively from the Jin and Tang era, when landscape was seen as a sum of isolated modules, into a much more sophisticated vision in which all elements were dissolved in pure space. In *The Mind Landscape of Xie Youy*, from the late 1380s, Zhao draws on the old idiom of green-and-blue, but grafts onto it a brushstroke the color of iron wire and a script in the seal style. The painting is no longer conceived as a representation of places, but of forms. It is elevated to the level of calligraphy, breaking up into a harmonious collection of calligraphic strokes, ink tones, and compositions created by earlier artists. In another celebrated scroll, *Autumn Colors on the Qiao and Hua Mountains* of 1296, Zhao Mengfu experiments with the use of the hemp-fiber

11

12

11. Zhou Tingqing, *The Amusement of Fish*, detail, Yuan dynasty, 1291, 12.1x233.7 in (30.8x593.7 cm). New York, Metropolitan Museum of Art.

12. Zhao Mengfu, *Horseman*, Yuan dynasty. Paris, Musée National des Arts Asiatiques-Guimet.

282

brushstroke in painting. He chooses to emphasize the calligraphic line, at the cost of a marked flattening of depth. He lingers on the relationship between extremes; the mountain on the right has an almost triangular shape (exalting the Point, the Acute), explicitly contrasted with the flattened and uniform one of the massif on the left (a plateau *par excellence*).

In *Villa on the Water*, of 1302, the ink is kept "thick," i.e. not very dilute, so that it picks up every imperfection in the paper, and is used to create a material effect, rather like in the medium of charcoal.

Working under the pseudonym of Songxuedaoren, "Taoist of the Snow on the Pine," he not only painted landscapes in pale, porous strokes, produced with an almost dry brush, but swamped the market with his pictures of horses. Some critics have seen these often unbridled colts as a metaphor for Chinese intellectuals, yearning to free themselves of the Mongol yoke. Many of the "horses" that have come down to us and are attributed to Zhao are in reality fakes, produced to meet the demands of collectors. We are told by a Zen monk called Osen Keishan that as early as the 15th century the ambassadors of Korea and Japan wanted to buy up his works.

Zhao justly boasted; "Every member of my family is a skilled painter or calligrapher." His most talented pupil was his wife, Guan Daosheng, who became a great painter of bamboo. She was born in 1262 and died in the 1320s.

According to his biographers, Qian Xuan was an alcoholic. Born at

14

13. Facing page: Zhao Menfgu, *Bamboo, Dry Tree and Rock*, Yuan dynasty.

14. Zhao Mengfu, *Autumn Colors on the Qiao and Hua Mountains*, detail, Yuan dynasty, 1293, 11x36.6 in, (28x93 cm). Taipei, National Palace Museum.

Huzhou and dying around 1275, he led the life of a hermit in the south. Admirers of his work used to take advantage of his drunken state to carry off his sketches, which they then had completed by forgers; as a result, the market was full of inauthentic works in his own lifetime. He was even obliged to change his signature to avoid forgery.

In *Wang Xizhi Watching Geese*, the great calligrapher of the 4th century is shown admiring the birds that are supposed to have inspired his writing, which was of legendary vigor. Qian Xuan used a *gongbi* style (a meticulous brushstroke, considered an amateurish, hyperrealistic approach, not that of a scholar). He had studied the masters of previous centuries so thoroughly that he once borrowed a painting of ducks, copied it overnight, then placed his copy in the original picture's mount and gave it back to its owner, who noticed nothing. He also liked to portray famous personages of the past, as in his *Taizu of the Song Dynasty Playing Football*. Today he is better known for his "flowers and birds;" his squirrels, insects, turtle doves and eggplants look like the real thing.

15

16

15. Qian Xuan, *Wang Xizhi Watching Geese*, detail, Yuan dynasty, about 1295, 9.1 x 36.5 in (23.2 x 92.7 cm). New York, Metropolitan Museum of Art.

16. Qian Xuan, *Flowers*, Yuan dynasty. Washington, Freer Gallery of Art, Smithsonian Institution.

**17. Qian Xuan, *Young
Nobleman on Horseback*,
Yuan dynasty, 1290.
London, British Museum.**

FOUR TITANS

Under the Mongol dynasty a change in patronage emerged that proved fairly traumatic for artists. Their clients were no longer courtiers, but members of the new landowning middle class. The figure of the emperor as the sole arbiter of taste was a thing of the past. However, even the Yuan produced royal patrons, such as Wenzong or Sengge, "dowager princess of the state of Lu." As if this were not enough, the irregular schedule of imperial competitions for officials left scholars without resources. However, the lack of employment for intellectuals had its positive aspects. Like ostriches lifting their heads at last from the sand, many learned scions of landowning families turned their attention to local oral traditions; they began to listen to the stewards and laborers who worked their farms. Various popular legends were written down for the first time in this period, which also saw a considerable development of the theater. One of the most inspired painters of the 14th century, Huang Gongwang, was a prolific playwright too. Huang was one of the "four masters" who are regarded as key figures in the art of this time, the others being Ni Zan, Wu Zhen and Wang Meng. They did not all know each other personally, as there

was no elite circle of acquaintances like the Su Shi group in the Song era. Nonetheless, they were all key figures in the intellectual resistance to Yuan rule, Jiangnan (the region of Nanjing). They preferred to paint on paper, a medium which required greater ability since, unlike silk, it could not be prepared with alum and thus absorbed the ink at once, leaving no room for second thoughts. In general their compositions were simplified and clear, and they thought of landscape painting as a visual poem, represented by figurative symbols. Man as an intermediary with nature tended to disappear from the paintings; all that was left at most was a caotang, a straw hut, to indicate the possible presence of an observer, who preferred to remain out of sight. But we have already seen that Qian Xuan, at the beginning of the dynasty, had yet to renounce the human figure, and the last of the great Yuan masters, Wang Meng, who in fact survived to see the birth of the Ming dynasty, never excluded country folk from his pictures. They are gripped by a *horror vacui* that is the exact opposite of the simplicity advocated earlier. In addition, the work of the four masters can be misleading; it is not representative of the choices made by most Yuan artists, who on the whole continued along the lines of Song academicism.

One of the outstanding members of this second generation of Yuan

18

18. Anonymous, *Portrait of Ni Zan*, Yuan dynasty, about 1340, 11.1x24 in (28.2x60.9 cm). Taipei, National Palace Museum.

19. Facing page: Wang Meng, *Grotto in the Forest of Juqu*, detail, Yuan dynasty. Taipei, National Palace Museum.

20

21

22

20-22. Huang Gongwang,
Dwelling in the Fuchun
Mountains, Yuan dynasty,
about 1350, 13x274 in
(33x696 cm). Taipei,
National Palace Museum.

artists was a former child prodigy, raised by adoptive parents and perhaps a pupil of Zhao Mengfu himself; Huang Gongwang (1269-1354). Adopted by the ninety-year-old Huang Le, he embarked on a dazzling career in the civil service, cut short all too soon by a scandal in 1315, for which he served a short time in prison. He ended up earning his living as a teacher of the "three religions" (Confucianism, Buddhism and Taoism) and a diviner, founding a school of philosophy at Suzhou. He spent his last seven to eight years in the Fuchun Mountains, living in huts that provided little shelter from the wind and rain. He used to sit and recite poetry, contemplating the mouth of the Mao River, or climb onto the roof to study how to paint clouds. It was there that he painted, over the course of four years, the scroll entitled *Dwelling* *in the Fuchun Mountains*. He was around eighty when he began this project. Even more amazing is his strict avoidance of color, transfiguring reality into a range of grays. Most of his paintings were ink monochromes, and when he did use colored pigments, he preferred to alternate between black and light purple, rather than the traditional green and blue. In *Clearing after Sudden Snow*, the mountain seems to draw back with the clouds and retreat to the right side of the painting; in the empty space left behind, the painter places a red circle, tiny but all the more powerful because it the only element of color in the composition; the sun setting over the snow. We can only wonder whether the object that vanishes under its light, at bottom left, is a mountain or a cloud. A friend, Dao Zongyi, collected his thoughts in an

23

**23. Wu Zhen, *Album*
of Ink Bamboo, detail,
Yuan dynasty, 1350. Taipei,
National Palace Museum.**

essay, *Xie Shanshui Jue* ("Secrets of Landscape Painting"). In it Huang offers tips on the use of colors, drawing on years of experimentation. For example, to convey the sensation of summer in the mountains, it is better to keep the brush well inked and then pass over the first coat with *luoqing* (shell blue), so as to create the impression of lush vegetation. Then it is a good idea to strew the composition with pools, bays and springs of water, which lend a sense of vivacity to the whole. Another master of the 14th century, Wu Zhen (1280-1354), practiced divining in order to make ends meet. An expert swordsman in his youth and totally uninterested in a career in the bureaucracy, he lived in Jiaxing. He often included in his paintings the figure of a solitary fisherman peacefully carrying out his work on a river, awed by the beauty of the surrounding nature. In the vertical scroll *Winter Ducks among the Reeds*, now in Beijing, the usual fisherman – his boat laden with

24

25

24. Sheng Mou, *Noble Scholar in an Autumn Grove*, Yuan dynasty, end of 1340. Taipei, National Palace Museum.

25. Wu Zhen, *Fisherman Recluse on Lake Dongting*, Yuan dynasty, 1341. Taipei, National Palace Museum.

26

26. Sheng Mou, *Hermit
Fisherman in Autumn
Forest*, Yuan dynasty,
1349. New York, Nathan
Cummings Foundation.

fish-pots – occupies the lower part of the picture. The transparency
of the broad river bed is conveyed by the absence of ink, exploiting
the coat of alum on the silk and requiring the viewer to reconstruct it
in his mind's eye. An almost dry brush depicts the fisherman and his
craft in a very clear way, with the oar abruptly disappearing from sight;
we are left to imagine the water in which it is immersed.
The man has been surprised by two ducks suddenly taking wing, but
by the time he raises his eyes to look for them in what for us is the
left-hand side of the scroll, they have already moved to the right. In
doing so they carry with them our gaze, which is then swiftly lost
in the long vista of mountains in the background, stretching to the
horizon.
Wu Zhen lived next door to a professional painter, Sheng Mou. Customers used to arrive loaded with gifts for Sheng, but not for him.

Wang was even jeered at by his wife but, unruffled, he reassured her; "Twenty years hence it will not be so." He was right.

In less than four square feet of paper (his *Bamboo after Su Shi* measures 42.9 x 12.6 in (109 x 32 cm), Wu Zhen was able to carry out an operation of subtle skill and moving sensitivity. The title *Bamboo after Su Shi* is not just a formula. Su Shi was one of the greatest all-round artists of the Song dynasty. His works were held in such esteem by the emperor that they were immortalized on stone stelae scattered as models all over the empire. During Su Shi's brief exile following his impeachment at the Song court, these tablets were shattered. In the inscription on the painting, Wu recounts how he came across one of them while on an excursion. He was walking outside the gates of Huzhou in the spring of 1350; he was seventy-one at the time, and Su Shi had died 250 years earlier. The power of the image was so convincing that Wu Zhen long declared himself unable to paint anything else. A series of his pictures of bamboo plants of the most varied forms, accompanied by poems and later gathered in a single portfolio, dates from the middle of the 14th century. Glancing though its pages, the impression we get is of drafts of poems in visual form; the urgency of the poetry is turned into *ximo*, a *divertissement* in ink. As Wu himself put it; "When I start painting, I forget myself and the brush in my hand – but do not [craftsmen who are perhaps artists, like] the cook and the potter, do the same?"

Wang Meng (1308-85) was the grandson of Zhao Mengfu. Born at Wuxing, in Zhejiang, he was the youngest of the four masters. In *Dwelling in the Qingbian Mountains*, painted in 1366, the vertical monumentality of the composition accentuates the luminous backdrop against which the mountain profile is silhouetted; the mountains float like clouds. An inscription on this painting, by the great 16th-century connoisseur Dong Qichang, quotes words of appreciation from Ni Zan: "the force of Master Wang's brushstrokes is enough to lift a tripod." Ni Zan admired Wang Meng, and yet they could not have been more different. Ni projected his schematic ideas onto nature, whereas Wang Meng drew energy from nature itself. In his role as an official, Wang was assigned to the region of Shandong. The back of his office gave onto a three-story building with a panorama of Mount Taishan. In idle periods he painted the view from its terrace. It took him three years to finish the painting. Then one winter it snowed. Wang wanted to repaint the picture: to keep up with nature, he wanted to add snow. A friend tied the brush to the string of his bow, sprinkling it with white pigment. Plucking the string made it snow on the painting as well. Later the scroll was lost in a fire. While the other Yuan masters were

27. Wang Meng,
Dwelling in the Qingbian
***Mountains,* Yuan dynasty,**
1366. Shanghai, Shanghai
Museum.

both great painters and first-class poets, the poems Wang wrote on his paintings were less convincing, but he did give his compositions great vigor. In the painting *Ge Zhichuan Moving House*, which can be seen in Beijing, the energy of the lines of force (*longmo*, "dragon veins," the Chinese call them) immediately captures our gaze and pulls it upward. It runs through the painting like a powerful backbone, rising like a coiled serpent; along these "ridges of energy" Wang continually changes his brushstroke, never tiring our eyes and always following the same impetus. Out of this come landscapes infused with unusual energy and meaning; the rock takes on the semblance of an antediluvian creature.

Wang used the same composition in *Mountain Cottage in Autumn*, painted around 1368 and now in Taipei. Here the energy of the mountain crest is restrained by the opposing arcs of two bays; in one of them, at bottom right, the first figure is again (as in Wu Zhen) a fisherman, waiting for his net to fill. In this part of the picture the painter lingers over his portrayal of gentlemen relaxing in their homes, enjoying the river scenery and almost staring straight into our eyes, as if caught by a powerful zoom lens; in the other, a couple on a small boat arrive from "outside" the scroll, after a trip on the river. The drifting craft introduces a horizontal movement into what is otherwise a wholly vertical composition. Wang liked to create landscapes with an atmosphere of suffering and anguish, perhaps out of a sort of gloomy foresight; falsely accused of involvement in a conspiracy against the Ming in 1380, he died in prison five years later. His crime was spending time admiring paintings in the company of Hu Weiyong, treacherous prime minister of the emperor of the new dynasty, Hongwu.

Ni Zan, one of the richest landowners in the empire, assembled an enviable collection in his studio cum gallery, the Qingbike. Obsessed with hygiene, he kept a basin by his side so that he could wash before painting. He studied the works of Huang Gongwang, imitating his sparing use of ink but achieving an exceptional power in his compositions. He based his riverscapes on a very limited number of variants, in order to concentrate on the ink and the lines. The picture is usually divided into three planes: right in the foreground, a bank or islet covered with a few slender trees, in the middle a river, i.e. an empty space; another bank in the distance, from which rise gently rolling hills. The foreground and background share nothing in common; only the trees give the painting a visual harmony. In this rarefaction of space, his pictures take on an extraordinary luminosity: the vertical and horizontal "dragon veins" sketch a solid grid, while each detail is almost explosive. Ni Zan used a dry brush, held almost edgeways, the angling

28. Ni Zan, *Landscape with Inscriptions*, Yuan dynasty. London, Christie's Auction House.

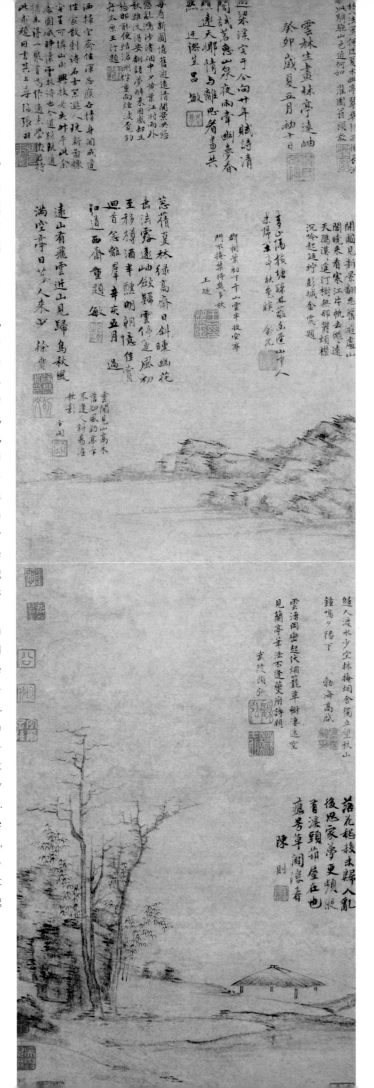

293

壬子歲七月五日雲林生寫

康賓市上懸盧未之詳甲寅三
月十四日懈郵舟復攜此畫來索
縣詩贈守仁仲醫師且錫山
不之故鄉則仁仲燕
居之小齋也月將歸故鄉登斯齋
持庖酒餞斯畫為仁仲壽當
遂吾志也雲林子識

鹿角東春風多杏花小齋容膝
庚年菲金梭躍水池魚戲彩鳳
柚林澗竹斜藿藿清談霏玉屑
蕭蕭白髮岸烏紗而今不二韓

allowing him to give things hard outlines, in complete contrast to Wu Zhen, who liked to blur his outlines. In the vertical scroll *Six Gentlemen*, painted in 1345, six tall trees stand on the island in the foreground, all different, each with its own foliage. The technique and title suggest fairly clearly that the six trees symbolize a group of intellectuals, gathered to contemplate the landscape; this painting offers a possible clue to the interpretation of Ni's other compositions. About sixty of his paintings have survived, but only a dozen are undoubtedly his own work. Yet Ni Zan left so many inscriptions that we can trace the movements and projects of the last twenty years of his life almost month by month; the worsening of his astigmatism can even be followed in the diagonals of his calligraphy, as slender and discreet as the trees in the silence of his panoramas. Born with the new century, by the age of fifty Ni had become very bitter about the heavy taxes extorted by the Mongol elite. Then he had an idea: given that the level of taxation was based on the amount of land he possessed, and sensing that popular discontent would lead to disturbances, he sold or rented all his plots of land. He did not even ask for immediate payment, telling the friends who bought from him that he would pick up the money at a later time. Everyone thought he was crazy, but he loaded his collection of paintings, a stock of silk scrolls and a plentiful supply of ink onto a boat and went to live on the region's many rivers. The Mongol tax collectors were no longer able to harass him as he lived on no land. Every so often he moored his boat, went to see a friend and collected part of the money he was owed, or stayed for a while and at the end, over a lavish meal, returned the favor by painting a masterpiece. Before long the countryside was devastated by the peasant revolts that were to bring the Ming dynasty to power, but Ni Zan now sailed calmly above the troubles of the time. As he wrote on one of his pictures, he painted "to give my feelings a home."

30

29. Facing page: Ni Zan, *The Rongxi Studio*, Yuan dynasty. Taipei, National Palace Museum.

30. Ni Zan, *Appreciating the Wilderness in an Autumn Grove*, Yuan dynasty, 1339. Private collection.

31. Ni Zan, *Six Gentlemen*, Yuan dynasty, 1345, 24.4x13.1 in (61.9x33.3 cm). Shanghai, Shanghai Museum.

THE WAYS OF DISSENT ARE MANY

The passion for modularity, for the repetition of a pattern, helped the revival of so-called "ruler-lined painting," i.e. of the architectural drawing. Xia Yong's *The Yellow Pavilion*, dating from around 1350, is of particular interest for its unabashed use of an inscription to balance the composition; the refined reproduction of an ancient *lishu* script of small dimensions is set in a central position, and in neatly lined ranks. The text is a poem written 200 years earlier, a lament over the suffering inflicted on peasants by floods. This would have immediately called to mind the natural disasters of 1344, which triggered popular discontent. The contrast could not have been more emphatic.

Wang Mian (1335-1415) was born at Kuaiji, in Zhejiang. The son of peasants, he contributed to the family budget as a child by working as a shepherd, but he was forced to reinvent himself on a number of occasions over the course of his life, eavesdropping at the village school instead of tending sheep. He soon entered a monastery, where he kept a lamp burning day and night so he could study as long as he wanted. Nevertheless he failed the exams for the civil service, then resolved to burn his writings and devote himself to learning the art of war. In the end he made his living teaching in an old temple. And painting plum trees. Only plum trees. Because they were a symbol of strength: they had the courage to announce the spring when there was still frost in the air. So there may have been a hint of anti-Mongol patriotism in his plums. It is said he once traveled to the north, to Hebei, to sell his paintings. On one scroll he dared to write; "Icy blossoms, one by one, clustering like jade; / The barbarian flute blows, but cannot blow them down."

Then he went home. He planted 1000 plum trees and 500 willows

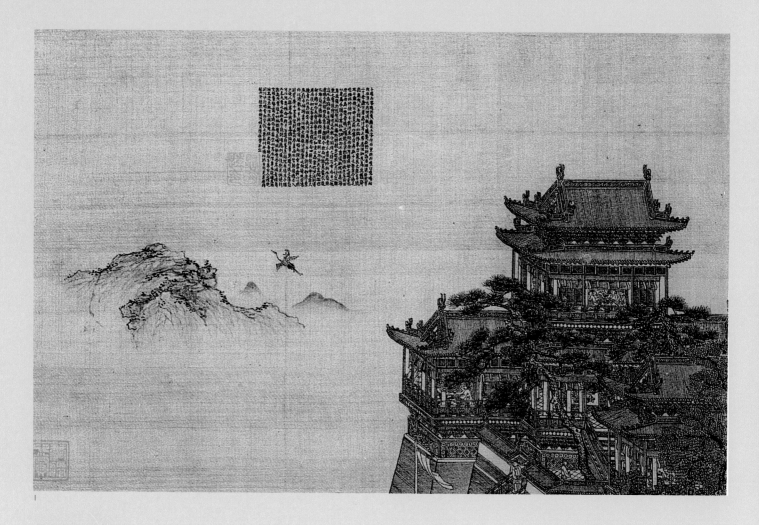

I. Xia Yong, *The Yellow Pavilion*, Yuan dynasty, about 1350, 8.1x10.6 in (20.7x26.8 cm). New York, Metropolitan Museum of Art.

and apricots. He built a little boat and went around, rather like Ni Zan,
bartering his paintings for fruit, so much paper for so many apples.

"The light of a silver moon trickles down

A pair of cranes dance in the night.

The sound of a flute from the south pavilion

would move a heart of stone, or of iron.

I would like to be like Chen Yuanlong [military leader of the three kingdoms,
Author's Note], who loaded his boat with pink crystals [cherries, Author's
Note], singing at the top of his voice, drunk, beating time to the rhythm of
the spring breezes and frightening an old man from Jiangnan, who fell to
the ground in a faint. 1415, on the eve of the harvest festival, the mountain
farmer from Kuaiji; Wang Mian."

It was the last thing he wrote.

II

III

II. Wang Mian, *Fragrant*
Snow at Broken Bridge,
detail, Yuan dynasty,
44.6x19.6 in (113.2x49.8 cm).
New York, Metropolitan
Museum of Art.

III. Wang Mian, *A Prunus*
in the Moonlight, **Yuan**
dynasty. Cleveland,
Museum of Art.

PORCELAIN? IT'S A PRODUCT OF THE EARTH...

The 14th century saw the supremacy of porcelain established. Kaolin and petuntse – its basic ingredients – were found in the natural world around the kilns of the new capital of the ceramics industry, Jingdezhen. The potters came up with another technological innovation, decoration in cobalt blue and red under a transparent glaze. Porcelain offers an ideal surface for painting; even before being placed in the kiln, even before receiving a glaze, it has a white and smooth surface. The vases took on unusual dimensions, and were covered with imposing figurative decorations. It is likely that the keenest customers were the numerous non-Chinese residents – Mongol rulers and foreign merchants – who had quite different tastes and bought the vases as objects for display (whence the growth in size) rather than for use. The cobalt (*sumali* in Chinese) came from Persia, where there was already an established tradition of pottery decorated in blue. But it was difficult to import Persian pieces along the caravan routes; instead it was easier to transport the raw materials and make the vases at home. The public adored the fact that, in competition with floral motifs, many vases were decorated with scenes from contemporary plays. The green of the famous Longquan glazes grew darker, and potters experimented with decorating by leaving unglazed some parts of the biscuit, which then turned brown on firing. The 14th century also heralded the importation of the technique of enamelwork, or cloisonné, from the Arabs, whereby the surface of the vase is divided into cloisons or "compartments," filled with enamel paste and then fired again. The compartments in which the enamel is set were cut into the clay after firing, or created prior to firing by the same mold from which the vase was cast. Initially

32

32. Tea caddy, Yuan dynasty. Fort Worth Kimbell Art Museum.

33. Facing page: *Meiping* vase for a branch of plum blossom, with incised decoration of dragons, Yuan dynasty, first half of 14th century. Fort Worth, Kimbell Art Museum.

this technique was used chiefly for the production of ceremonial vases for the rituals of Lamaist Buddhism, the religion embraced by the Mongols. The vase, the "core" of this procedure, could be made of stoneware or porcelain, but from the Ming period (the reign of Emperor Xuande) onward it was increasingly often made of metal. The Manchurian rulers of the Qing dynasty (1644-1910) admired this technique and the process became popular, also being used for the production of incense burners, flowerpots, small boxes, cups and fancy goods for women.

In the 18th century the aesthetic quality of the enamelwork went into decline, reverting to conventional motifs. Even in the 16th century simple geometric patterns were used to divide the large surfaces of the vases into smaller compartments. The first names of masters of lacquer workshops were recorded in books on the history of art, and this period saw the emergence of a new self-awareness among craftsmen. Even lacquered trays, like pottery, reached a size that was too large for practical use; the object became a pretext, a vehicle for the ornamentation. The work was painstaking: the lacquer, a resin derived from a tree, was applied to a base of wood and cloth, layer by layer, until it reached the required thickness for carving, in a technique called *diaoqi*. The layers could be of different colors, so that the carving revealed a shade that contrasted with the rest; the outer layer tended to be left brown, or preferably a deep red if the decoration was figured. In the later dynasties of the Ming and Qing, craftsmen applied as many as two hundred layers of lacquer, each one taking a day to be laid on and to dry. The process also had a devastating effect on the lungs of the lacquerers, who were forced to inhale the dust of orpiment, which is basically arsenic, and cinnabar, which is mercuric sulfide. However, no history of the art makes any mention of the poor health of these craftsmen.

34

34. Chun Incense burner, Yuan dynasty. New York, Granger Collection.

35. Facing page: Pumpkin-shaped vase in *celadon* ware, Yuan dynasty, 14th century. Bath, Museum of East Asian Art. Dried pumpkins were used as water bottles; this is a ceramic version of the same vessel, covered with magnificent crazing.

9. China under the Ming: Restoration and Innovation

Spanning three centuries (1368-1644), the Ming Dynasty is best known for the elegant porcelain that was manufactured in large quantities not just for the imperial court but also for the flourishing foreign market, which toward the end of the dynasty lay firmly in the hands of Portuguese merchants.

The emergence of a solid mercantile class within China itself stimulated significant production of luxury goods and works of art intended for the wealthier strata of society: the "consumption of art," from paintings to porcelain, from lacquered furniture to jade carvings, is one of the principal characteristics of this period. Yet in the field of painting, the highest Chinese art form, it was not a very creative time, with considerable repetition of styles and composition models typical of earlier dynasties.

1. Facing page: Bronze statue of Buddha, Ming dynasty. London, Christie's Auction House.

2. Lacquered plate with carved decoration, Ming dynasty, reign of the emperor Hongzhi (1487-1505), 1489. London, British Museum. It represents a famous meeting between scholars and poets that took place in the "Orchid Pavilion" in the 4th century.

THE BIRTH OF THE DYNASTY

In 1368, after a prolonged period of civil war, the throne of the Son of Heaven was again occupied by a dynasty of Chinese origin, which assumed the title of Ming, "The Bright." This was an implicit reference to the presumed period of obscurantism under long foreign rule and to the return to a brilliant civilization that was entirely Chinese in character. In truth, such an exalted dynastic title was little suited to the humble origins of its founder, Zhu Yuanzhang (1328-98), who began a beggar yet died an emperor. The son of peasants, he was orphaned as a child and became, in the interests of survival rather than out of piety, a monk in a Buddhist temple. Discovering that monastic life was not for him, he left the monastery and took to living on the road, eventually joining one of the many bands of brigands that plagued China in the years of transition and chaos that marked the end of Mongol rule.

Unlike other bandits and rebels, Zhu Yuanzhang did not limit himself to plundering and raiding but gradually conquered a number of territories. In 1356 he captured the city of Nanjing, which he made the capital of the small kingdom he set up in South China. In 1368, after defeating the other rebel leaders in the south of the country, he finally moved against Beijing, taking the city peacefully as the Mongol emperor had chosen to retreat to the northern territories. Ascending the throne under the dynastic name of Hongwu, Zhu Yuanzhang spent the next thirty years fighting the Mongols, who continued to attack the Chinese in an attempt to win back their lost empire. But the forces led by his highly capable and loyal general Xu Da reached deep into the heart of Central Asia where, in 1372, they put Karakorum, Genghis Khan's capital city, to the sword. A few years later, in 1381, the Mongols were also driven out of the southwestern province of Yunnan and the country was once again entirely in Chinese hands.

3

3. Large porcelain basin with floral decoration painted in red underglaze, Ming dynasty, period and mark of the reign of the emperor Hongwu (1368-98), diameter 16.3 in (41.3 cm). Taipei, National Palace Museum.

4. Facing page: Anonymous court painter, formal portrait of the founder of the Ming dynasty, the emperor Hongwu (reigned 1368-98), second half of 14th century. Taipei, National Palace Museum.

大明太祖高皇帝

5. Facing page: Four
ivory statuettes, three of
them representing Taoist
immortals (including
Zhongli Quan, considered
the most important of
the "Eight Immortals")

and one the bodhisattva
Guanyin, Ming dynasty.
Private collection.

6. Ornament for clothing
in openwork gold and
set with semiprecious
stones, Ming dynasty,
15th century. London,
British Museum. The
motif of dragons facing

one another across the
"flaming pearl,"
of Buddhist derivation,
suggests that the
ornament was probably
reserved for the emperor.

CHINA AS A SEA POWER

In the light of these events we can understand why one of the first preoccupations of the Ming rulers was the repair of the Great Wall (already extended during the Han dynasty), the enormous line of defense that crossed a large part of China. The Ming's most recent military operations had extended the borders of the empire further to the north than they had ever been under any previous dynasty. Yet the threat of invasion from the north remained and so it was necessary to take adequate protective measures. Despite having penetrated into Central Asia, however, the Ming dynasts were no longer interested in exercising direct control of those regions as the Tang before them had done. Instead, the Ming had been quick to grasp the important fact that the main routes of trade were by sea. China became a first-rate naval power under their rule, boasting a formidable fleet and admirals such as the eunuch Zhang who were

to make a significant impact in the field of exploration. For a people who were essentially land-based, the sea now became a familiar part of the Chinese world, to the extent that it even featured on ceramic wares. The porcelain produced during the reign of Emperor Xuande (1426-35), which is now housed at the Palace Museums of Beijing and Taipei, was frequently decorated with motifs of marine creatures of fantastic appearance.

The connection with the sea was also facilitated by the position of the capital Nanjing, conveniently located on the final stretch of the Yangtze or Yangzi River. The city was restructured to make it architecturally worthy of the status of imperial capital: its walls, stretching for over 12 miles (20 kilometers) and reaching a height of almost 65 feet (20 meters), are still the largest urban defense works in the world. In addition, even during the time that the Southern Song dynasty had been based in this region, it had ceased to be merely a source of food production – the fertility of the land was such that it could produce

7

**7. One of the stretches
of the Great Wall of China
near Mutianyu, after
reconstruction during
the Ming period.**

8. Blue and white porcelain goblet with decorative motifs in red representing fantastic sea creatures, Ming dynasty, reign of the emperor Xuande (1426-35), diameter 4 in (10.1 cm). Taipei, National Palace Museum.

three crops of rice a year when conditions were ideal – and had also prospered culturally. The main rivers used as trade routes passed through this region and brought to the coastal cities the precious cargoes of porcelain manufactured in industrial quantities in the kilns of Jingdezhen. A further advantage, and by no means an insignificant one, was that the city of Nanjing was protected geographically from possible incursions by the nomadic peoples of the north. However, none of these factors was taken into consideration by the Yongle emperor (1402-24), the third Ming ruler and usurper of the throne, when in 1420 he moved the capital of the empire back to Beijing. It was a move that was to eventually prove one of the main causes of the dynasty's weakening and, in the end, its fall.

The move back to Beijing necessitated renovation work on a large scale, which also affected the city's many temples as well as the seat of imperial power, the complex that is today known as the Forbidden City. Numerous workshops were set up in Beijing to manufacture decorative objects for the residences of the court and the imperial aristocracy. They employed craftsmen brought in from other centers of production located in the south of the country. One of the most important of these workshops was the so-called Orchid Factory, not a place for the cultivation of flowers, as the name might imply, but for the production of the lacquered objects that are still regarded today as one of the glories of Ming decorative arts. Hundreds of layers of lacquer were applied to a wooden core and, once dry, carved in such a way as to create a decoration with a three-dimensional effect, a technique that had been practiced in China ever since the time of the Southern Song in the prosperous urban centers situated near the mouth of the Yangzi.

10

9. Facing page: *Cloisonné* vase with wide lid, decorated with dragons on a background of clouds, Ming dynasty, reign of the emperor Xuande (1426-35). London, British Museum.

10. View of the *Qiang Qing Men*, the "Gate of Heavenly Purity," 15th century. Beijing, Forbidden City. This was the main entrance to the inner courtyard, which constituted the private section of the Forbidden City where the emperors of the Ming and Qing dynasties resided.

THE ARTS UNDER THE MING

Comparing works of painting and calligraphy, the nobler arts that were practiced by the literati during the long period of Ming rule, to those produced during the earlier Song dynasty, the results seem disappointing. The work inevitably seems repetitive, sometimes even tired and devoid of any real innovative force.

If we then look at the fields of poetry and philosophy as well, areas in which previous dynasties had excelled, the Ming only seem at best imitators of what the Chinese "genius" had created in the past. So why then is the name of this dynasty so inextricably linked with Chinese art, to the extent that "Ming" has become almost synonymous with the highest and most sophisticated artistic production of that civilization? It has to be a wholly Western point of view, prompted by the large numbers of Chinese artifacts that were imported into Europe under the Ming dynasty and resulting from the increase in trade with Europe from the 16th century onward. Portuguese merchants were allowed to settle at Macao (1517) and ships loaded with porcelain sailed from China twice a year, some of the cargoes being sold in the markets of Asia and some taken into Lisbon, where it was sold on to European buyers.

As a result, Europe began to develop an appreciation of Chinese art through the porcelain that was being imported, which was certainly one of the finest products of the Ming period.

11

11. Circular ink tablet decorated with the auspicious motif called *baizitu* (as the inscription also states), i.e. the motif "of the hundred children," signed by the craftsman **Cheng Junfang, Ming dynasty, 1604. Tianjin, Tianjin Art Museum.**

12. Silver drinking cup signed by Zhu Bishan and representing a Taoist sage, Ming dynasty, 15th century, length 9.3 in (23.6 cm). Taipei, National Palace Museum.

13

13. *Dehua* porcelain statuette representing Cai Shen, the god of prosperity: an inscription on the base dates it to the 37th year of the reign of the emperor Wanli of the Ming dynasty, i.e. 1610. London, British Museum.

14. Facing page: *Sancai* ("three-color") ceramic statuette representing the fat and smiling monk Budai, Ming dynasty, 1486. London, British Museum.

PORCELAIN AND FOREIGN TRADE

The Ming emperors began adding reign marks to the objects produced, especially those made of porcelain, a practice that would be continued by the Qing, dynasty that succeeded them. These artifacts were manufactured for the court under the strict control of the imperial officials who acted as supervisors at the factories. The concept of "signature" also took on greater importance under the Ming than it had in earlier periods; from the 16th century onward, any artist who wished his painting to acquire the status of a "work of art" had to make sure that it was signed in order for it to attain the value it merited on the flourishing domestic art market. The craftsmen who produced the accessories and equipment that were indispensable for painting, the highest form of art, also signed their work. We therefore know the names of some of the people who made the stones on which the ink was ground, the carved brush holders made from bamboo or fine wood, and of those who polished the jade that adorned the studies of the scholars of the period.

It is of great benefit to the contextualization of the work that is necessary for historical and artistic study. The marks on porcelain, produced in quantity in the southern kilns of Jingdezhen, which could guarantee the best results thanks to the quality of the raw materials, are fairly standardized and can be summed up in formulas of six characters, or ideograms, such as *Da Ming Xuande nian zhi*, or "Produced (*zhi*) in the reign (*nian*) of the Xuande emperor (*Xuande*) of the great (*da*) Ming dynasty." This practice was also connected with the fact that in the early part of the dynasty an imperial decree prohibited foreign trade, although it had played an important part in the economy of the previous Yuan dynasty. However, porcelain and precious silks were used as gifts when diplomatic exchanges with other countries began to increase. We know from official inventories that in the year 1383 alone some 19,000 pieces of porcelain were sent abroad as official gifts. Floral motifs predominated in terms of decorative subject matter. Painted in red underglaze, they consisted chiefly of the flowers that symbolized the four seasons: the peony for spring, apple blossom for summer, the chrysanthemum

16

15. Facing page: Blue and white porcelain bowl, Ming dynasty, period and mark of the reign of the emperor Xuande (1426-35). Private collection.

16. Porcelain bowl with red copper glaze and scalloped rim, Ming dynasty, reign of the emperor Xuande (1426-35). Beijing, Palace Museum.

17-18. Following pages: Red porcelain bowl decorated with floral motifs, Ming dynasty, 16th century. Bath, Museum of East Asian Art, and porcelain vase decorated

with figures of dragons, Ming dynasty, reign of the emperor Jiajing (1521-67). Berlin, Museum für Ostasiatische Kunst.

PAINTING

Despite the high instance of repetition in Ming painting, it would be completely wrong to consider the painting of this time as worthless and totally lacking in an expressive force of its own. It was inevitable, however, that the achievements of the acknowledged "giants" of Chinese painting of earlier periods would be followed by a period of relative stagnation, and this is what in fact happened.

During this "pause for reflection" the figure of the critic and theoretician Dong Qichang (1555-1636) stands out. It is he who must be thanked for having put the history of Chinese art in perspective, in an overview that had a profound impact on posterity and even on the thinking of some Western scholars.

His ideas, often reduced to formulas that do not do justice to the complexity of his arguments, have only recently been subjected to precise and meticulous critical scrutiny, placing his work in its correct historical perspective. A wealthy scholar who held some of the highest official posts, he owned one of the largest collections of art ever assembled. He had a deep understanding of the Buddhist and philosophical tradition, as well as being a skilled calligrapher and highly regarded painter in his own right, his pictures being much sought after by his contemporaries.

This appreciation for the works produced by contemporary artists led to the development of a flourishing domestic art market from the 15th century onward, reflecting the rising level of wealth and the presence of a solid mercantile class as well as prosperous intellectuals.

The tomb of the merchant Wang Zhen (1425-95) at Huaian, in Jiangsu province produced ample evidence of this. When excavated it yielded a work of calligraphy and a total of twenty-four paintings, mounted together in one long scroll, signed by recognized artists of the period. Analysis by modern scholars, however, has revealed that two of the pictures Wang Zhen believed to have been painted by Yuan artists were fakes, perhaps an inevitable consequence of the thriving trade in antiquities at that time. The proliferation of works of doubtful authenticity was certainly abetted by the widespread use of templates made from carved wood used for the printing of texts and illustrations during the Ming period. As a result, images that were once limited to the narrow circle of court artists circulated much more widely, allowing skillful "craftsmen" to learn styles and iconographies and so imitate acknowledged masters of the past in deliberate forgeries.

22. Dong Qichang, *In the Shade of Summer Trees*, Ming dynasty, 1635. Taipei, National Palace Museum.

All this generated a lively debate over the role of the artist in Chinese society, leading to a differentiation between "genuine" artists, i.e. those who painted and practiced calligraphy not for financial gain but as a means of improving themselves and the culture to which they belonged, and the so-called "professional" artists who instead traded on their skills, earning a living by the sale of their work. This dichotomy found expression, obviously, among the upper classes of society, who supported painting as a noble art ideologically along Confucian lines, but it found little echo in the artistic practice of the time, as scholars and painters of repute were sometimes obliged to sell some of their works in order to cope with financial difficulties.

The emperors were undoubtedly among those who could permit themselves the luxury of cultivating "art for art's sake." One of them, Xuande, is regarded by Chinese critics as the most artistically gifted of the Chinese rulers, along with the Song emperor Huizong (1100-25).

Xuande modeled much of his painting style on that of his illustrious predecessor, and also followed his example in acting as a patron of artists and scholars when he decided to revive the prestigious Song institution of the Imperial Academy of Fine Arts.

One of Xuande's most highly regarded works is the scroll *Gibbons at Play*, painted during the second year of his reign. It was inspired by a theme popular among professional painters and Buddhists because of the complex symbolism with which the image of the gibbon, or the monkey in general, was associated in China. In addition to being one of the animals featured in the Chinese Zodiac, the monkey was for Buddhists a symbol of the human race itself, and the expression *sanyuan*, "three gibbons," was synonymous with "triple success." Xuande's painting therefore was a perfect gift to be presented to an official of the court on the occasion of his rise in rank. Many of the pictures that the emperor painted were in fact donated by him in

23

23. Shen Zhou (1427-1509),
Drawings from Life, **Ming**
dynasty, 1494, 13.7x21.8 in
(34.7x55.4 cm). Taipei,
National Palace Museum.

24

24. Emperor Xuande,
Gibbons at Play, Ming
dynasty, 1427. Taipei,
National Palace Museum.

such circumstances, partly as a means of strengthening his ties with the men who occupied positions of trust in his entourage. From a stylistic viewpoint, the painting is also filled with references to techniques adopted by masters of the past: for instance, the technique used in the shading and modeling of the rocks and tree trunks, as well as in the depiction of the bamboo plants, alludes explicitly to the brushwork of the great master of the Yuan period, Li Kan (1254-1320).

25

26

25. Zhang Lu, Lao-tzu *Riding a Buffalo*, Ming dynasty, 40x21.8 in (101.5x55.3 cm). Taipei, National Palace Museum. Many of the surviving works of Zhang Lu, leading artist of the group known as the "Zhejiang school," are of Taoist subjects like this one, where Lao-tzu is shown, as tradition relates, leaving China astride a buffalo.

26. Zhu Duan, *Reciting Poems in a Courtyard of Pines*, Ming dynasty, first half of 16th century. Tianjin, Tianjin Art Museum.

GARDENS AND PRIVATE HOMES

Among the more highly acclaimed professional painters of the period it is worth mentioning Qiu Ying (about 1494-1552), so famous that his works were forged while he was still alive. One of his best-known paintings depicts the garden of an elegant and exclusive residence, where the master of the house waits at the threshold to welcome the guest who has come to pay him a visit.

The painting is a perfect illustration of the domestic and private setting that provided a backdrop for much of the cultural life of the literati and artists of Southern China. It also reflects the intimate cultivation and appreciation of nature that found their highest expression in gardening, an art which reached its peak under the Ming dynasty. The garden became the preeminent "luxury" of the time, partly because landed property was the primary source of wealth and the yardstick by which the prosperity of an individual or a family could be measured. Unfortunately, the gardens that can still be admired today in the cities of the south such as Suzhou have been totally transformed, and nothing but the name remains of the original. To get an idea of what Ming gardens must have looked like we have to turn to the "representation" of them that can be found in the painting and literature of the period. It is from these sources – the most outstanding of the literary works being Wen Zhenheng's (1585-1645) *Treatise on Superfluous Things* – that we learn of the care that was taken to turn a limited and defined

27

28

326

27. View of a garden, Ming dynasty. Suzhou.

28. Qiu Ying, *The Garden of Wang Chuan's Villa*, in the style of the artist Wang Wei (701-61), Ming dynasty. Private collection. Known as one of the "four masters of Suzhou," Qiu Ying was noted for his landscapes painted in the "green-and-blue" style of the Tang dynasty.

space into a microcosm of nature. Plants, trees, rock formations, pools and watercourses, paths and architectural elements, were all composed in a harmonious and coherent visual whole in order to communicate the *idea* of nature that Chinese scholars had pursued so tenaciously since the first landscape paintings. In other words, rather than being a place where nature was appreciated for itself, the garden became an entity that encapsulated both the Confucian and Taoist values that the scholars embodied in their person and expressed in their art. It was both a place for the spirit, used in private as a source of inspiration for the artist and man of letters, and a setting in which the same man, in a more public arena, acted as a representative of the highest and noblest ideals of the tradition.

To understand this concept better we can look at one of the many paintings of the Ming era in which this setting, with its protagonist the *wenren*, the man of letters, is depicted faithfully. This is the scroll entitled *Enjoying Antiquities* signed by Du Jin (about 1465-1509), which portrays one of the pastimes that was most typical of the intellectual pleasures of the Ming scholar, the study of works of art in the peace and quiet of his private garden. It is evident that the picture has been composed to convey the idealized image of the perfect "gentleman" who, in the company of an equally cultivated friend, passes his free time in the study of artifacts symbolic of Chinese civilization. On the table at the center of the picture are a large number of bronze ritual vessels dating from the ancient Shang and Zhou dynasties, set alongside elegant examples of Song pottery; on another table, where several painted scrolls are arranged neatly, two attendants are placing a zither (*qin*), still wrapped in its silk covering – it will be played by the two scholars at the end of their afternoon of study. A boy enters the scene from the left carrying a chessboard: the game of chess, music, calligraphy, and painting were the four noble arts in which the perfect scholar was expected to be well versed. The plants depicted at the rear are some of those favored by the Chinese in their gardens – bamboo, plane, cypress and *wutong* – while the elaborate rock in the foreground reminds us that the stones shaped by natural forces and found at the bottom of Lake Tai, in Southern China, constituted an essential element of garden ornament. The significance of the composition is made even more explicit by the inscription that the artist has traced in the top left corner of the painting, in which he celebrates the importance of a life ordered in accordance with the dictates of ritual and music, and devoted to the study, appreciation and practice of art. *(F. S.)*

29. Qiu Ying, *Two scholars Playing the Qin and Erhu under a Pine,* **Ming dynasty. Private collection.**

10. The Qing and the End of the Chinese Empire

The Qing dynasty brought to an end the long history of the Chinese Empire, a history which had begun in 221 BCE with the first unification of the country by Qin Shi Huangdi and now ended with the country under foreign rule once more.

However, the Manchurian origins of the Qing did not prevent the enlightened emperors of the period from assuming the role of interpreters and defenders of Chinese culture, literature, poetry, and art. It is thanks to emperors like Qianlong who collected thousands of works over the course of their lives that we can still admire precious treasures from the Chinese past. The open-mindedness of the Qing rulers is also confirmed by their interest in European culture. The most famous example is the Italian Jesuit Giuseppe Castiglione, who spent fifty years at the court painting pictures that fascinated Qianlong through their use of Western techniques, cleverly combined with the elements of classical Chinese painting. Castiglione's influence was to last a long time and led to oil painting being regularly practiced in Chinese schools of art from the 19th century onward.

1. Facing page: Porcelain vase with polychrome enameled decoration and a motif of stylized dragons in the openwork central part, Qing dynasty, reign of the emperor Qianlong (1736-96). Taipei, National Palace Museum.

2. Jade pendant in the form of a dragon, Qing dynasty, 18th-19th century. London, British Museum.

THE ORIGINS

Although historical dates can often create the impression that one dynasty ended at a given moment and another took its place, in reality things are not so simple. In China such changes were rarely sudden, but instead involved long periods of political, economic, and cultural instability that characterized the final phase of a dynasty. These periods were then followed by many more years, often decades, of consolidation of the new ruler's power. This is exactly what happened between the end of the Ming and the installation on the throne of the Qing. This dynasty marked the end of the long impe-

rial age that began in the 3rd century BCE and came formally to a close with the abdication, on February 12, 1912, of the last emperor, Puyi, celebrated in Bertolucci's film of the same name. The slow decline of the Ming commenced around 1600, with frequent raids by Japanese pirates on the coasts, the growth of European settlements in the coastal cities, and the harassment of the Tatars who, beyond the line of defense represented by the Great Wall, were establishing themselves as a state in the land of Manchuria, corresponding to the modern northeastern provinces of Liaoning, Heilongjiang and Jilin. However, it was not this range of external factors that brought about the collapse of the Ming dynasty, but internal struggles be-

3

3. Interior of the imperial palace. Shenyang.

tween factions of the aristocracy over possession of the imperial throne, and the growing number of rebellions that were breaking out in the country. While the China of the Ming slowly crumbled, the Manchu had plenty of time to prepare themselves, militarily and politically. In 1616, their leader Nurhaci (1559-1626) stopped the regular payment of tribute to the Ming court and founded the Jin dynasty. The Manchu then commenced a gradual erosion of the northern territories under Chinese control, and in 1626 set up their capital at Mukden, now Shenyang (Liaoning province). Today, it is still possible to visit the imperial palace in Mukden, whose layout echoes that of the Forbidden City in Beijing, residence of the Ming emper-

ors. The Qing dynasty, whose name means "The Pure," was formally established in 1636, three years prior to a massive invasion of China. In the meantime, the rebel Li Zheng marched on the capital with his own army, arriving beneath the walls of Beijing in 1644. Seeing himself lost, the last Ming emperor, Chong Zhen, committed suicide by hanging himself from a tree. This was the signal for the Manchu: under the pretext of punishing the rebels who had caused the death of the Ming sovereign and claiming to have the mandate of Heaven to rule the country, they marched on the capital, defeated Li Zheng and installed Fulin on the throne. Under the name of Shunzhi (1644-61), he became the first Qing emperor of China.

4

4. View of the Forbidden City from above. Beijing.

6

5. Facing page: Anonymous court artist, from the *Twelve Beauties at Leisure*, painting on silk, Qing dynasty, late Kangxi period, 1709-23. Beijing, Palace Museum.

The painting depicts one of the favorites of Prince Yinzhen, who was to become emperor under the name of Yongzheng.

6. Imperial *longpao*, or "dragon robe," Qing dynasty, reign of the emperor Qianlong. Palace Museum, Beijing. The silk robe is embroidered with motifs symbolizing imperial authority, especially the five-clawed dragons.

BARBARIANS AND CHINESE

For a long time the Manchurian troops had to fight against pockets of strong resistance in various regions of the country by people who clearly did not want to see foreign rulers occupy once more the throne of the Son of Heaven. Despite the gradual subjugation of the whole country, this loyalty to the Ming dynasty represented the most painful slight to the Manchu sovereigns, yet at the same time the greatest stimulus to their increasing sinicization. This process also had major repercussions in the field of culture and art, turning the Qing emperors into fervent admirers and patrons of Chinese culture. They became supporters and practitioners of the arts, open to contacts

7

7. "Gate of the Presentation of Congratulations." Beijing, Forbidden City. This is the entrance to the building where the winners of state competitions were officially recognized. All the palaces and halls that make up the architectural complex of the Forbidden City have their names written in Manchu characters on the left and in Chinese ones on the right.

with other civilizations, as well as ardent collectors, excellent poets, and skilled calligraphers. Paradoxically, the deliberate process of acculturation meant that they became more Chinese than the Chinese, but they never renounced their own ethnic, cultural and linguistic roots. This is clear from the dual system of writing, Manchu and Chinese, adopted in official documents, from details of their clothing, from their architecture, and from their choice of particular iconographic motifs. They were enlightened rulers able to bring about a synthesis between different traditions, at least on the level of official culture and art. They could inject new lifeblood into Chinese artistic production, with results that were to reverberate in China for centuries to come, and in some ways, right down to the present day.

8

8. Huang Ren, stone for grinding ink, Qing dynasty, reign of the emperor Kangxi (1662-1722). Tianjin, Tianjin Art Museum.

9

9. Anonymous court
artist, *Portrait of Emperor
Kangxi at His Desk*,
Qing dynasty, reign
of the emperor Kangxi.
Beijing, Palace Museum.

10. Brush holder made from a section of bamboo and carved with the scene of the "Seven Sages of the Bamboo Grove," Qing dynasty, late 17th century - early 18th century. Taipei, National Palace Museum.

THREE ENLIGHTENED EMPERORS

Three emperors were responsible for this long and delicate process of cultural synthesis, three rulers whose imposing figures still stand out against the backdrop of Chinese history: Kangxi (1661-1722), Yongzheng (1722-35) and Qianlong (1736-96). Kangxi was just eight when he ascended the throne and remained on it for sixty-one years. He completed the task of unifying China, fought the inevitable enemies within the court, and devoted himself to making peace between Chinese and Manchu in order to strengthen the state. To this end he promoted new imperial competitions to encourage the recruitment of scholars who were reluctant to collaborate with the new ruling house. Perhaps it was to convey how much he admired Chinese history and culture that he ordered the compilation of an official history of the Ming dynasty, and of the biggest dictionary ever to have been completed in China. The *Kangxi Zidian*, which bears his name, is a lexicon of over 40,000 ideograms or characters. He also showed himself well disposed to the Christian missionaries who had arrived on European ships the previous century (Matteo Ricci had set foot in China in 1581), and with an edict of tolerance in 1690 authorized them to build churches all over the country. However, the question of rites, that is to say whether Chinese converts would be allowed to continue practicing the cult of their ancestors, whom they venerated with images and tablets on altars in their homes, led the Church of Rome to adopt an intransigent position. As a result, in 1706, Kangxi revoked the missionaries' freedom to propagate their faith. Yet the basis for a dialogue, at least on the cultural plane, had been laid some time earlier and certainly could not be canceled out from one day to the next. The Qing emperors were genuinely interested in Western culture, science and art. As early as the 17th century, the Jesuits had commenced a major undertaking, the translation of fundamental texts of the Western tradition into Chinese. At the same time, they brought the bases of the Chinese cultural edifice to the attention of Europeans, through their translation into Latin of the Confucian classics. It was in this climate of cultural openness and mutual curiosity and interest that the figure of the Italian artist Giuseppe Castiglione emerged.

12

11. Facing page: Anonymous court artist, *Portrait of Emperor Kangxi*, Qing dynasty, end of the reign of the emperor Kangxi, early 18th century. Beijing, Palace Museum.

12. Container for perfumes in carved bamboo, Qing dynasty, reign of the emperor Qianlong. Tianjin, Tianjin Art Museum.

13. Following pages: Block of jade carved with the auspicious motif of the "Nine Elders of Huichang," Qing dynasty, reign of the emperor Qianlong.

Palace Museum, Beijing. The scene refers to the poet Bo Juyi and his friends who, at the age of over eighty, met in the spring of 845 to celebrate their longevity; and

Giuseppe Castiglione (Lang Shining), *Spring's Peaceful Message*, Qing dynasty, reign of the emperor Qianlong, 1736. Beijing, Palace Museum. The painting on silk was

executed to celebrate the ascent of Emperor Qianlong to the throne.

写真世宁擅缋我少
年时入宝皤然者不
知此是谁
壬寅暮春沈毛

GIUSEPPE CASTIGLIONE: A JESUIT PAINTER AT THE COURT OF THE QING DYNASTY

The saying "no one is a prophet in his own land" can aptly be applied to Giuseppe Castiglione (1688-1766), a priest of the Society of Jesus. Before setting off for China, where he lived for the rest of his life, Castiglione was trained in the art of painting by another Jesuit, Andrea Pozzo (1642-1709), author of the treatise *Perspectiva Pictorum et Architectorum*, subsequently translated into Chinese. This preparation must have proved useful for creating Christian images and religious icons with

which to adorn the churches that were being built in China. But fate had something different in store for Castiglione, and he ended up becoming a painter and artist at the imperial court for half a century, during which time he "served" under three emperors, the aforementioned Kangxi as well as Yongzheng and Qianlong. He has gone down in history under his Chinese name, Lang Shining. It all started when he was presented at court in 1715 by other Jesuits living in Beijing, although only a few of them had access to the Forbidden City, where they acted chiefly in the capacity of experts on science and mathematics. It was probably his use of Western techniques of painting that roused the curiosity of the emperors, who commissioned numerous paintings from Castiglione, many

15. Giuseppe Castiglione (Lang Shining), *The Emperor Qianlong out Hunting,* **Qing dynasty, reign of the emperor Qianlong, 1755. Beijing, Palace Museum.**

16. Facing page: Giuseppe Castiglione (Lang Shining), *Pine, Hawk and Glossy Ganoderma,* **Qing dynasty, reign of the emperor Qianlong,**

1724. Beijing, Palace Museum. The painting, with auspicious motifs (the glossy ganoderma is also known as the mushroom of immortality),

was presented by the Italian Jesuit to Emperor Qianlong on his birthday.

CHINESE ART

of which are still in the imperial collections, now split between Beijing and Taipei. They included formal portraits of the sovereigns wearing their sumptuous imperial robes embroidered with the symbols of their authority, the dragon in particular; long scrolls with vivid depictions of the great hunts carried out in the territories to the north, of the military campaigns conducted by the Qing in the regions of the northwest or of the imperial journeys to the south of China. There were also celebratory paintings offered to the rulers on special occasions, such as their birthdays, and filled with auspicious symbols drawn from the Chinese tradition, and portraits of Emperor Qianlong's favorite horses and hounds, even of his concubines. This last is a fact of great interest since contact with the emperor's wives was forbidden to men and permitted, inside the walls of the Forbidden City, only to eunuchs. Castiglione's success has to be ascribed to his capacity to fuse techniques derived from Western painting and extraneous to the Chinese tradition of art – such as the application of perspective when representing architecture, the use of chiaroscuro, and the ability to render volume in portraiture – with traditional Chinese modes of composition and stylistic approaches to the handling of natural subjects and views of the landscape. The skill he displayed also earned the Italian painter the opportunity to tackle the "design" of many of the objects that adorned the imperial residences, from fine porcelain vases to bronze vessels enameled and decorated with the *cloisonné* technique. Finally, he became the architect of the Yuanmingyuan, the Western-style palaces Emperor Qianlong had built in a vast section of the imperial park situated in the northeastern suburbs of Beijing. In the fifty years he spent at the court, Castiglione was able to refine his understanding of Chinese techniques of painting, based on the adroit use of brush and ink. Yet the emperor Qianlong felt that these remained unsurpassed even in the face of the Italian artist's undisputed skill, as he chose to emphasize in an inscription written on one of the Jesuit's paintings. But Castiglione also instructed Chinese painters in the use of Western techniques, in particular oil painting, whose effects on canvas the artist learned how to reproduce fairly closely through the superimposition of several layers of silk or paper.

The Jesuit's influence would be fundamental to the adoption of oil painting in China. Initially used to produce paintings acquired by Western travelers in the port cities of Southern China, it became the "official" technique in the 20th century, when Mao's China showed a preference for the use of oil in pictures celebrating the Chinese Revolution and inspired by the socialist realism of the Soviet Union.

17

17. Giuseppe Castiglione (Lang Shining), *The Mulan Hunt,* **1742, 19.3x5.9 in (49x15 cm). Paris, Musée National des Arts Asiatiques-Guimet.**

18. Ruins of the Western-
style palaces that
Emperor Qianlong of the
Qing dynasty had built to
the design of Giuseppe
Castiglione and other
Jesuits. Beijing.

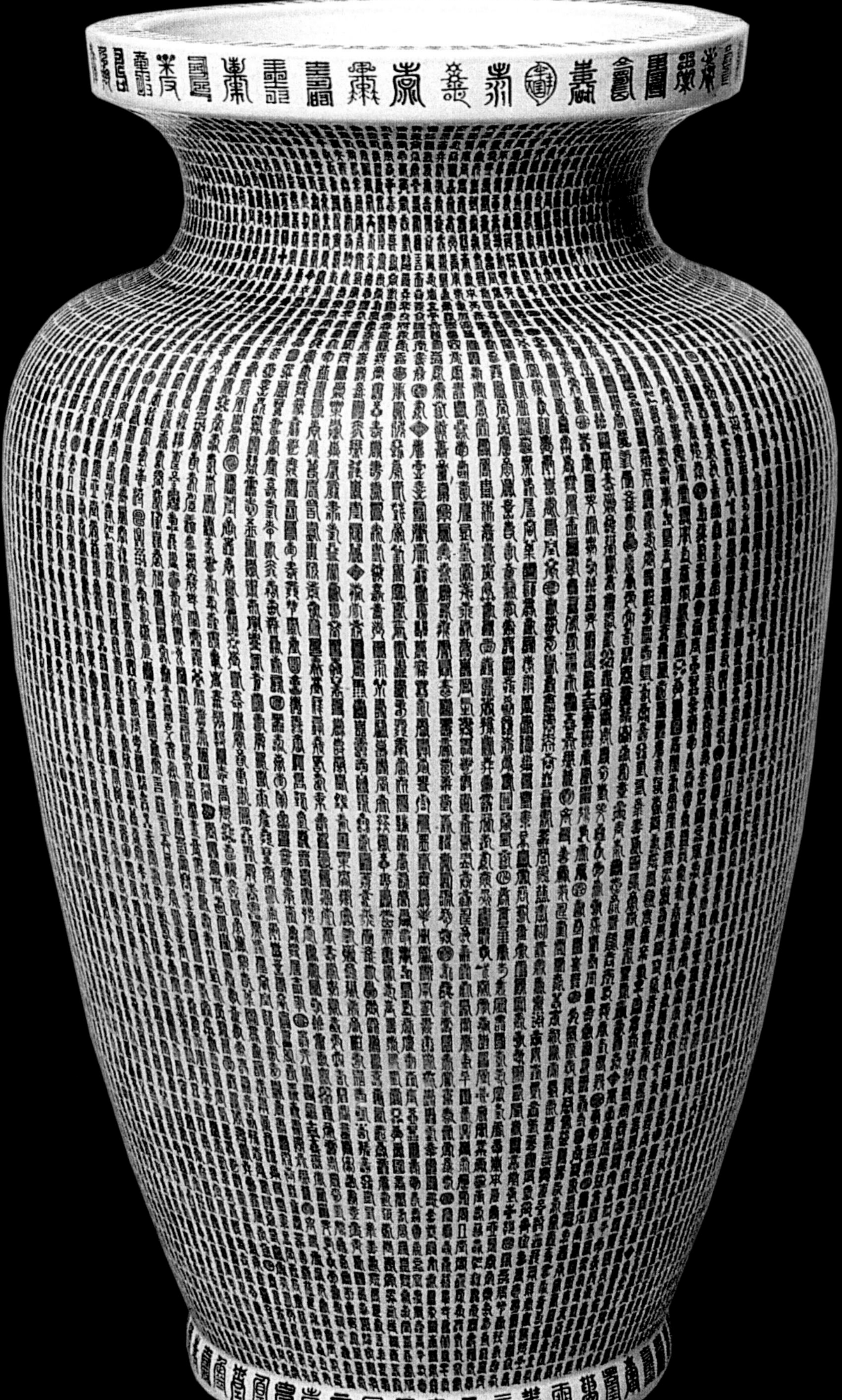

Castiglione's influence on the circle of artists and intellectuals at the Qing court did not diminish the status of the traditional arts. On the contrary, these received the enthusiastic patronage of the new rulers once they had concluded their campaign of conquest of China. The kilns of Jingdezhen, where the finest porcelain was produced, no doubt experienced a downturn in the long period of transition between the end of the Ming and the beginning of the Qing, when they were actually rebuilt, in 1677. Six kilns were devoted to the production of crockery for the court, but this was no longer marked with the name of the emperor (considered too sacred to be placed on objects that were basically of everyday use, however refined they may have been). The emperor's mark was now replaced by appropri-

20

19. Facing page: Porcelain vase from the Jingdezhen kilns (Jiangxi province) decorated with the character *shou,* "longevity," repeated over the entire surface of the object, Qing dynasty, reign of the emperor Kangxi, height 13.8 in (35 cm). Beijing, Palace Museum.

20. Porcelain table mat with underglaze cobalt blue decoration, from the Jingdezhen kilns (Jiangxi province), Qing dynasty, reign of the emperor Jiaqing (1796-1820). London, British Museum.

ate symbols like shells and a variety of flowers. According to tradition, this practice was introduced by the supervisor of imperial production, Zhang Qizhong, but it was not always followed, as is seen in examples that have survived, such as bowls with enameled decoration bearing the reign marks of Kangxi and Yongzheng. Even production for export flourished anew. White and blue porcelain accounted for the lion's share, but it was accompanied by models alien to the Chinese tradition and made expressly for European markets. Craftsmen skilled in the carving of jade, bamboo, wood and stone intensified their production of instruments and accessories for writing, such as brushes, brush rests and brush holders, ink tablets, small screens for the table, elbow rests, lacquered boxes, and desks. The studies of the literati were now adorned, as they had been at the time of the Ming, with jade sculptures representing the abodes of the immortals, or landscapes in miniature, placed alongside lacquered containers for writing implements. Throughout the 18th century, China under the Qing saw a flourishing output, which reflected the extraordinary skills of Chinese craftsmen but was not always satisfying from the viewpoint of taste. This was due to an excess of ornamentation pervaded by a sense of *horror vacui*, all too affected in its obsessive attention to detail and excessive in its use of images adorning the artifacts. It was a style diametrically opposed to the simplicity of Song sobriety.

This excessive decoration is also to be found in the architecture of the palaces, concentrated for the most part in the capital, Beijing. It is seen in the emperor's chair in the Taihedian, the Hall of Supreme Harmony also known as the Throne Room, recently brought back to its original splendor by an Italian team of restorers. It is also evident in the wooden beams painted with genre scenes and landscapes echoing the gentle scenery of South China that were used to construct the open corridors running around the large pool of water in the Summer Palace, and in the iconographic superfluity and lavish coloring of the capital's Buddhist temples. In short, while Qing art seems to have been heir to the best Chinese tradition, this legacy was distorted, perhaps precisely because of the influence of that Manchurian background – and its slightly barbaric flavor, Chinese purists would add – which the Qing rulers were never willing to renounce completely.

21

21. Imperial porcelain
bowl decorated with
auspicious floral motifs
and a poem, Qing dynasty,
period and mark of the
reign of the emperor
Yongzheng (1722-1735).
Beijing, Palace Museum.

22. Porcelain teapot with
monochrome *celadon*
glaze, Qing dynasty,
period and mark of the
reign of the emperor
Yongzheng. Beijing,
Palace Museum.

IMPERIAL PORCELAIN BOWL WITH ENAMELED FLORAL DECORATION

Qing dynasty, reign of the emperor Yongzheng (1722-35)
diameter: 4.3 in (10.8 cm)
Taipei, National Palace Museum

The absolute perfection in the execution of this extremely delicate porcelain bowl is typical of the highly sophisticated articles produced by the Jingdezhen kilns for the imperial family. In this case the bowl was made for Emperor Yongzheng, as we are told by the mark painted in blue ink on the bottom and outside, in a script inspired by the one that was in use during the Song period.

The object is covered on the inside and outside with a brilliant white glaze devoid of imperfections. Over this, and on the outside, has been applied a thin layer of yellow enamel, the symbolic color of the emperor, while two extremely narrow bands have been left uncovered at the bottom of the low ring-shaped foot and on the slightly flared rim.

The motifs, also painted in polychrome enamel, are drawn from the natural world – blades of grass, rocks, fungi, orchids, hawthorn. They convey a symbolic message of good luck and longevity, made explicit by a short poem inscribed on the side of the bowl not in view, which runs: "*Down there, on that island of jade wreathed in distant clouds, live the immortals; in the warmth of spring, the orchids fill the air with their scent.*"

Jade, orchids, spring, the immortals – to whose elixirs of longevity the twisted fungi that sprout from the rock are a clear reference – are all images evoking long life, good health and reinvigoration of the body and spirit.

The perfection of the object and the message it carries suggest that the bowl was commissioned to celebrate the birthday of Emperor Yong-zheng. The body of the bowl was made at Jingdezhen, but the enameled decoration was added subsequently in the specialized workshops of Bei-jing, which operated under direct imperial supervision.

EMPEROR QIANLONG, THE COLLECTOR

The Emperor Qianlong was more generous in his patronage of the arts than any before him, possibly because of his foreign origins and his desire to appear to his subjects as the genuine interpreter and heir of the Chinese cultural tradition. He became one of the most avid collectors of artistic artifacts recorded in Chinese history, giving his seal of approval to countless objects of great craftsmanship by allowing their makers to mark them with his name and the period of his reign.

The specialized workshops run under imperial supervision, often lo-

cated near the Forbidden City, produced so many artifacts in the most varied materials — lacquer, jade, wood, glass, metal — that even today counterfeiters often use spurious marks. The aim is to give an aura of credibility to their creations and pass them off as antiques — a practice already widespread in the 19th century — by attributing them to the period of the Emperor Qianlong's reign. However, it is one thing to promote the development of the arts and crafts and quite another to collect works of art, at least from the viewpoint of the classical Chinese tradition. Possessing objects from the past — a custom that in China we can with certainty trace back to the Han dynasty at least — signified

23

24

352

23. Porcelain vase decorated with floral patterns, Qing dynasty, period and mark of the reign of the emperor Qianlong, perhaps from the imperial collections **of the Summer Palace in Beijing, height 13.8 in (35 cm). Paris, Musée National des Arts Asiatiques-Guimet.** **24. Enameled porcelain snuffbox with European-style decoration, Qing dynasty, reign of the emperor Qianlong. Private collection.**

25

25. Bronze ritual vessel
of the *gui* type adorned with
dragons motifs, dynasty of
the Western Zhou, 10th-9th
century BCE, height 8.4 in
(21.3 cm), formerly in the
imperial collections.
Taipei, National Palace
Museum.

entering into direct contact with one's cultural roots and thus becoming a repository of culture itself, as well as a guarantor of its transmission to subsequent generations. In the case of the emperors, this assumed particular importance because of their position on the highest rung of society and therefore their role as custodians *par excellence* of the "treasures" handed down to them.

Where the Qing emperors, of Manchurian origin, were concerned, this took on an additional significance: as foreigners, it was vital that they were not seen for as damaging the rich Chinese culture with all its values, but protecting, encouraging, reinvigorating, and preserving it for posterity. In this Emperor Qianlong was extremely successful; if today we can admire precious and rare examples of painting and calligraphy dating from ancient dynasties like the Song, or even earlier periods, we owe it to his zeal as a collector. Despite the devastating upheavals that marked the history of China in the 19th and 20th centuries, the imperial collections have been preserved to a large extent, although they are now divided between Beijing and Taipei, capitals of the "two Chinas," the People's and Nationalist Republics, created over the course of the last century. In order to gain recognition as a "connoisseur of the subject" by the Chinese intellectuals who made up the class of imperial bureaucrats and officials, Qianlong spent many years studying classical Chinese culture. In doing so, he revealed a personal penchant for collecting that led him to amass bronzes of the old dynasties, jades from the Neolithic and Han periods, valuable specimens of calligraphy and painting and refined porcelain from the Song and Ming periods. This was never, however, collecting for its own sake, but to show that Qianlong was watching over the illustrious Chinese past with an expert eye. The objects were not merely an appendage to his authority but were an integral part of the image of himself that the sovereign wanted to present to his contemporaries and to posterity. To emphasize his appreciation, the emperor often composed poems celebrating the beauty and quality of a work of art. The poems, written in his own hand in elegant calligraphy, were then

26

354

26. Ink stone, Song dynasty. It is decorated with the motif of the "Orchid Pavilion," an allusion to the place which inspired the calligrapher Wang **Xizhi (4th century CE) to write the text that was to become one of the "classics" of the art of calligraphy.**

transcribed by faithful copyists onto the works themselves. They were engraved on the polished surface of ancient jades, painted on refined pieces of porcelain, and carved into antique bronzes.

When the works in question were on silk and paper, we can be sure the celebratory inscriptions were often written by the emperor himself, as his name can be read in the red imprints of the imperial seals that were stamped on the work to mark his ownership. Such a practice might appear a sacrilege in Western eyes, violating the work by intervening directly on it through the affixing of inscriptions and seals. But in ancient China this was precisely what confirmed the antiquity and value of a painting or piece of calligraphy. The appreciation of posterity, transcribed on the work itself, only served to enhance its value and the position of high prestige it occupied in Chinese culture.

In any case, the passion for antiques was deeply felt and widespread among the Qing intelligentsia, and found expression not just in collecting but also in the reassessment to which traditional arts like calligraphy were subjected. In fact a growing skepticism toward the erudite tradition led to a closer examination of the ancient classics and to the rediscovery of now disused styles of writing, often identified on stone stelae and in inscriptions in tombs, on ancient monuments and on rocks in the mountains. This work played an important part in the development of the antiquarian studies that led to modern archeological research, in the sense of a systematic investigation of the past. This was just one of the many new elements that enriched the cultural panorama of the late Qing period, along with the increasing influence of Western culture and of internal currents of thought. While one of the biggest upheavals to have taken place in Chinese history, that of the Taiping Rebellion (1851-64), marked the beginning of the dynasty's decline, a new China was about to emerge on the world stage: a China that, while not totally repudiating its own cultural and artistic past, now embarked upon the journey of research and experimentation that was to lead to its contemporary production of art. (F. S.)

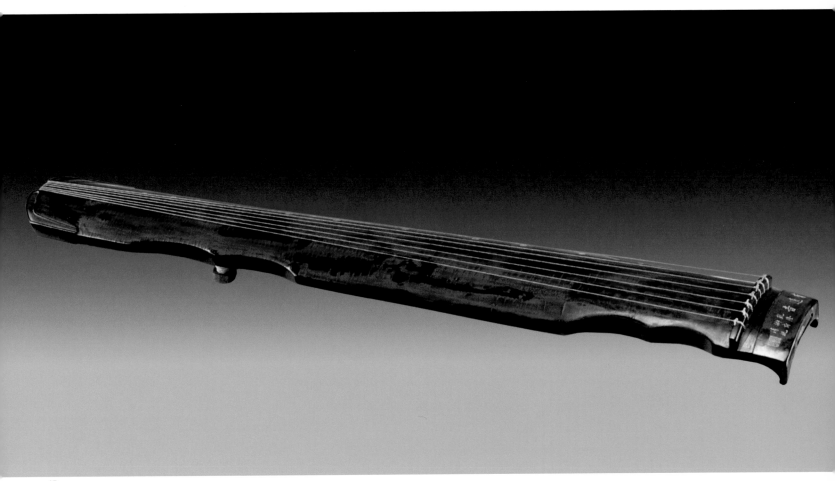

27. Stringed instrument known as the "Chinese zither" and called the *Wanhe songtao*, lacquered wood with gold and jade inserts, Song dynasty.

CHRONOLOGY

7000-2000 BCE NEOLITHIC

· Communities settled in villages all over the territory; numerous cultural horizons can be distinguished by their different production of pottery.
· Around 6000-5000 BCE there is the first evidence of the working of jade.

3000-2000 3000-2000 BCE Late Neolithic

· Increasing level of social complexity in some cultures, Liangzhu (about 3300-2200 BCE) and Longshan (about 3000-1700 BCE), with elaborate graves containing ritual artifacts in jade.
· Evidence for the use of lacquer around 3000 BCE.

PERIOD OF THE THREE DYNASTIES

Xia Dynasty (?)

· The actual existence of this dynasty has not yet been demonstrated by epigraphic evidence; it is traditionally dated to between 2205 and 1766 BCE.

About 1500-1050 BCE Shang dynasty

· Earliest evidence of writing from the site of the last capital, Anyang. Development of bronzework, society ruled by the king and aristocracy.

About 1200 BCE

· The finds at Sanxingdui and tomb of the queen Fu Hao, at Anyang.

About 1050-221 BCE Zhou dynasty

About 1050-770 BCE Western Zhou

· The Zhou kingdom is governed on the basis of a system of assignment and administration of territories known as "Chinese feudalism."
· The production of bronzes continues, with the inscriptions on the vessels growing longer and becoming invaluable sources of historical information.
· The earliest texts of ancient Chinese literature appear: the *Book of Odes* is composed sometime between 900 and 600 BCE.

770-221 BCE Eastern Zhou

· The central authority loses its hold on local lords and a phase of internal divisions begins that is traditionally known by the names of its two sub-periods, "Spring and Autumn" (770-475 BCE) and "Warring States" (475-221 BCE).
· First schools of thought: Confucius lives from circa 551 to 479 BCE while the canonical text of Taoism, the Tao-te Ching (Daodejing, "The Book of the Way and Its Virtue") is written sometime between 400 and 200 BCE.

THE FIRST EMPIRE

221-207 BCE Qin dynasty

· The Qin kingdom annexes the other small states into which the territory of China is divided and in 221 BCE the country is unified.
· The First Emperor, Qin Shi Huangdi, orders the construction – in the vicinity of modern Xian, where his capital is located – of his mausoleum, guarded by an army of terracotta soldiers, the first evidence of ancient statuary.
· Systematization of writing.

206 BCE-220 CE Han dynasty

· The capital is located at Chang'an, now Xian, and subsequently moved to Luoyang. The dynasty is then split into the Western Han (206 BCE-8 CE) and Eastern Han (25-220 CE), with an interregnum caused by Wang Mang's usurpation of the throne, which led to the foundation of the short-lived Xin dynasty (9-23 CE).
· Around 100 BCE paper is invented and the first dictionary of the Chinese language compiled.
· Around 100 BCE the Buddhist religion arrives in China.

Period of disunity

· The fall of the Han dynasty is followed by around four centuries of disunity in the country, with numerous independent dynasties, often of short duration, founded all over the country.

Three Kingdoms

· Wei 220-65.
· Shu (Han) 221-263.
· Wu 222-280.
· Commanding personal armies, three generals divide up the empire into as many areas, the north, the lower basin of the Yangzi River and Sichuan. The power of the military leaders has to reckon with the emerging class of landowners.

265-420 Jin dynasty

· Western Jin 265-316.
· Eastern Jin 317-420.
· The calligraphers Wang Xizhi (about 309-65), Wang Xianzhi (344-88) and Wang Xun (350-401) create their masterpieces, and the painter Gu Kaizhi (about 345 - circa 406) is active at the Jin court.
· Sixteen Kingdoms (in the north) 304-420.

420-589 Southern and Northern Dynasties

South

· Liu Song 420-479.
· Southern Qi 479-502.
· Liang 502-557.
· Chen 557-589.

North

· Northern or Later Wei 386-535.
· The main caves in the Buddhist complex of Yungang are created.
· Eastern Wei 534-50.
· Western Wei 535-56.
· Northern Qi 550-77.
· Northern Zhou 557-81.

· Nomadic peoples settle in the northern territory of China, creating institutions that are a hybrid of tribal and Chinese traditions.
· Buddhism is the official religion of the Wei royal house, which funds the creation of complexes of cave temples near its capitals.
· The earliest cave in the Dunhuang complex, in the province of Gansu, dates from 538-39.
· Xie He, author of the *Six Principles of Painting*, is active from circa 500 to circa 535.

THE MIDDLE EMPIRE

581-618 Sui dynasty

· The construction of a canal linking the northern catchment basin with the Yangzi River is begun in 589. With unification the potters of the northern and southern kilns are able to compare their technological advances and porcelain is discovered around 600.

618-907 Tang dynasty

· With the conquests in Central Asia the territory of China reaches its largest extent. Trade and cultural exchange flourish along the routes of the Silk Road.
· The cosmopolitan capital of the Tang, Chang'an, is the largest and most populous city in the Asia of the time and is home to foreign princes and ambassadors, as well as artists and merchants from all over the world. Freedom of worship and religious tolerance is widespread and an elite of cultured and learned officials is recruited through the imperial examinations.
· The rebellion by the general of Sogdian origin, An Lushan, in 754 marks the beginning of the dynasty's decline.
· From 750 onward printing with woodblocks is developed and classical poetry reaches its peak with Li Bai (fl. 701-62) and Du Fu (fl. 712-70).
· Buddhism flourishes despite the persecution of the years 845-47: in 868 the Diamond Sūtra is printed and in 874 the crypt of the pagoda in the Famen Temple at Xi'an is sealed.

907-960 Five Dynasties

· On the abdication of the last Tang emperor, Aizong, the country falls into political anarchy and breaks up into eleven different states. Nonetheless there are great developments in art thanks to the work of painters like Dong Yuan, who dies in 962.

THE LATE EMPIRE

907-1125 Liao dynasty

· The north of the country falls into the hands of a dynasty of foreign origin whose importance has recently been reassessed thanks to archeological discoveries and historical and artistic studies.

960-1279 Song dynasty

960-1127 Northern Song

· Capital at Kaifeng.

1127-1279 Southern Song

· Capital at Hangzhou.
· Scientific, naturalistic, mathematical and mechanical studies flourish.
· It is the golden age of the "flowers and birds" genre of painting, one of the whose most able exponents turns out to be the emperor Huizong (1082-1135).
· Nomadic peoples exercise pressure on the borders: the prosperous court of the Middle Kingdom buys peace by paying tribute, but first has to transfer its capital (1127-1278), ceding pieces of land to the "barbarians." It is then swept away forever by the largest empire in history, that of the Mongol Khan.

While the Chinese court retreats south, the north of the country sees the emergence of the dynasties:

1032-1227 Western Xia dynasty

1115-1234 Jin dynasty

1276-1368 Yuan dynasty

· The Mongols conquer China as well and move the capital of their empire to Beijing. They soon yield to the allure of Chinese culture. They retreat in the face of a series of peasant revolts in the 1360s.
· First development and export of blue and white porcelain.

1368-1644 Ming dynasty

· Capitals at Nanjing ("southern capital") and Beijing ("northern capital").
· A thriving network of local market towns emerges in the 17th century.
· The increase in the scale of manufacturing is not accompanied by an adequate development of technology: the market for the export of silk and porcelain expands thanks to European merchants.
· On his voyages Admiral Zheng He perhaps discovers the American continent before Christopher Columbus, but China remains indifferent to his explorations.

1644-1911 Qing dynasty

· Beijing is the capital. The ruling Manchu win the favor of the elite of officials. Thanks to this pact between classes, China experiences substantial social peace throughout the 18th century and develops an intense network of cultural exchanges with Europe through the mediation of the Jesuits: the Italian painter Giuseppe Castiglione (1688-1766) is active at court.
· In the 19th century, a financial crisis, economic recession and rampant corruption in the ruling class trigger devastating social revolts between 1850 and 1870. Pressure from the Western powers and Japan (which unlike China embarks on a decisive modernization around 1870) leads the empire toward collapse.
· The last emperor, Puyi, abdicates on February 12, 1912.

BIBLIOGRAPHY

For an overview of Chinese civilization and developments in the artistic field the reader is referred to the following texts:

CRAIG CLUNAS, *Art in China*. Oxford e New York: Oxford University Press, 1997.
A clear and concise introduction to the history of art in China: it stands out for its thematic approach to the subject and for its accurate contextualization of the works.

GABRIELE FAHR-BECKER (ed.), *The Art of East Asia*. Colonia: Könemann, 2000.
Lavishly illustrated volume: in addition to the section devoted to China, there are chapters on calligraphy and jade.

MICHÈLE PIRAZZOLI-T'SERSTEVENS (ed.), *La Cina*, 2 vols. Turin, Utet, 1996.
This work in Italian offers a wide-ranging vision of the development of Far Eastern civilization, with particular attention paid to art.

LAURENCE SICKMAN e ALEXANDER SOPER ALEXANDER, *The Art and Architecture of China*. Baltimore: Penguin Books, 1956.
A work devoted to architecture, it remains unsurpassed for the accuracy of its treatment and the breadth of the material examined.

MICHAEL SULLIVAN, *The Arts of China*. Berkeley: University of California Press, 1984.
A classic text on the subject, but not updated to take account of the latest advances in knowledge, especially with regard to the archeological discoveries made after the data of its publication.

On the archeological discoveries that have radically changed our understanding of the Chinese past:

XIAONENG YANG, *The Golden Age of Chinese Archaeology. Celebrated Discoveries from the People's Republic of China*. Washington: National Gallery of Art, 1999.
Catalogue of the biggest exhibition staged in recent years and focused on the results achieved by Chinese archeology over around a century of activity. Periods from the Neolithic to the Tang dynasty are illustrated in detail through 175 exhibits selected from all the principal Chinese museums and set in their context in descriptions compiled by a group of twenty-four Chinese and Western experts.

On painting and calligraphy:

OSVALD SIRÉN, *Chinese Painting: Leading Masters and Principles*. Londra: Lund Humphries; New York, Ronald Press Co., 1956-1958.
Although not a recent publication, the volume still constitutes one of the best means of finding one's bearings in the ocean of Chinese painting.

JAMES CAHILL, *The Painter's Practice: How Artists Lived and Worked in Traditional China*. New York: Columbia University Press, 1994.
The American scholar, who has taught at the University of Berkeley, California, has led the studies that have revolutionized our approach to the understanding of Chinese painting over the last fifteen years.

JAMES CAHILL, *Three Alternative Histories of Chinese Painting*. Lawrence, Kansas: Spencer Museum of Art, University of Kansas, 1988.
A personal reconsideration by the author of some of the canonical theories that have long dominated the field in the West, it is brilliant and acute like the majority of writings by this great scholar.

WEN C. FONG, *Beyond Representation: Chinese Painting and Calligraphy, 8th-14th century.* New York:Metropolitan Museum of Art; New Haven, Yale University Press, 1992.
Written by one of the most famous Chinese-American experts on Chinese painting, the volume focuses principally on an analysis of the works in New York's Metropolitan Museum.

On jade:

JESSICA RAWSON, *Chinese Jade. From the Neolithic to the Qing.* Londra: British Museum Press, 1995.
Currently the most complete treatment of jade in China, from ancient times up to the last imperial dynasty, structured in the form of a catalogue illustrating Sir Joseph Hotung's collection of jade, part of which has been donated to the British Museum.

FILIPPO SALVIATI, *The Language of Adornment. Chinese Ornaments of Jade, Crystal, Amber and Glass.* Paris: Myrna Myers, 2002.
A history and explanation of the symbolic meanings of the recurrent decorative motifs on objects of personal ornamentation made out of jade and other materials in ancient China, with particular reference to the Liao period and based on the specimens present in the Myers collection.

Catalogues of exhibitions of Chinese art held in Italy:

7000 anni di Cina. Milan: Silvana Editoriale, 1983.
Catalogue of the first major exhibition held in Venice and devoted to the initial phase of development of the Chinese civilization, from the Neolithic period to the Han dynasty.

D. HAR and J. DE DIANA (eds.), *China in Venice: From the Han dynasty to Marco Polo.* Milan: Electa, 1986.
Ideal continuation of the preceding exhibition with artifacts illustrating Chinese art up until the Song period, and thus shortly before the arrival of the Venetian merchant in China.

ROBERTO CIARLA (ed.) *Cina 220 a.C. I guerrieri di Xi'an.* Milan: Cataloghi, Abitare Segesta, 1994.
Catalogue of the monographic exhibition held in Italy and centering on some of the soldiers of the terracotta army found at Lintong, Xian, in 1974.

LUCIA CATERINA and GIOVANNI VERARDI (eds.), *Tang. Arte e cultura in Cina prima dell'anno Mille.* Milan: Electa, 2005.
Monographic exhibition devoted to the great Tang dynasty with finds made by the Italian archeologists who have carried out the excavations on the site of an important Buddhist monastery of the period.

On the China of the period Qing:

EVELYN S. RAWSKI and JESSICA RAWSON (eds.), *China, The Three Emperors, 1662-1795.* London: Royal Academy of Arts, 2005.
Catalogue of the exhibition of the same name held at the Royal Academy of Arts in London and centering on the figures and work of three Qing emperors, Kangxi (1661-1722), Yongzheng (1722-35) and Qianlong (1736-96), through artifacts in the imperial collections conserved in the Palace Museum inside the Forbidden City in Beijing.